The aftermath of the 2008 earthquake in Sichuan, China.

THE BIG ONE

THE CASCADIA EARTHQUAKES AND THE SCIENCE OF SAVING LIVES

ELIZABETH RUSCH

Houghton Mifflin Harcourt
Boston   New York

To all the scientists working to keep us safe

hmhbooks.com

The illustrations in this book were done digitally in Procreate.
The text type was set in Garamond MT Std.
The display type was set in Knockout.

Design by Nina Simoneaux and Andrea Miller

Library of Congress Cataloging-in-Publication Data

Names: Rusch, Elizabeth, author.
Title: The big one : the Cascadia earthquakes and the science of saving lives / Elizabeth Rusch.
Other titles: Cascadia earthquakes and the science of saving lives
Description: Boston : Houghton Mifflin Harcourt, 2020. | Series: Scientists in the field | Audience: Age 10–12. | Audience: Grade 4 to 6. | Includes bibliographical references.
Identifiers: LCCN 2019016728 | ISBN 9780544889040 (hardcover)
Subjects: LCSH: Cascadia Subduction Zone—Juvenile literature. | Earthquakes—Northwest, Pacific—Juvenile literature. | Earthquake prediction—Northwest, Pacific—Juvenile literature. | Plate tectonics—Northwest, Pacific—Juvenile literature. | Plate tectonics—Juvenile literature. | Earthquake zones—Northwest Coast of North America—Juvenile literature. | Subduction zones—Northwest Coast of North America—Juvenile literature. Classification: LCC QE535.2.N6 R87 2020 | DDC 551.2209795—dc23
LC record available at https://lccn.loc.gov/2019016728

Manufactured in China
SCP 10 9 8 7 6 5 4 3 2 1
4500798255

Photo Credits can be found on page 73.

The damage to a new office building in the city of Concepción, Chile, wrought by the 8.8 magnitude earthquake in 2010.

TABLE OF CONTENTS

A bus crash that occurred during the 8.0 magnitude earthquake in Sichuan, China, in May 2008.

PROLOGUE

THE BIG ONE

AT FIRST YOU DON'T NOTICE THE SHAKING. You think a bus or truck is rumbling by. But the trembling doesn't stop. A few seconds later, paintings and photos on the wall swing slightly. Glasses and dishes rattle. *Thud. Bang!* Objects all around you—cellphones, water bottles, books—slide off surfaces and clatter to the ground. Within a minute, the floor beneath your feet heaves as the rumble becomes louder and louder. You dive under a table and hug one of the legs tightly as a window shatters. Couches, chairs, and cabinets pitch back and forth. A heavy desk jiggles across the room as a bookshelf lurches, then leans and topples.

Outside, trees bend back and forth as if their trunks were made of elastic. Skyscrapers sway like reeds. Sidewalks and roads ripple and heave. People lose their footing and stumble to their knees as the rumble becomes a roar. Roof tiles crash, chimneys disintegrate, and walls begin to crack, crumble, and collapse.

Two minutes into the earthquake, the entire 620-mile (1,000-kilometer) stretch of the Pacific Northwest of the United States and Canada undulates. The shaking reaches millions of people, from Vancouver, British Columbia, through Seattle, Washington, and Portland, Oregon, all the way down to Mendocino, California.

But the powerful trembling has only just begun. While most earthquakes last about ten to thirty seconds, this earthquake, called a Cascadia earthquake, could last three to six minutes.

How long is six minutes? Long enough to play two songs on the radio. Long enough to drain a full bathtub a couple of times. Long enough to destroy roads, bridges, schools, and hospitals; derail trains and damage power and fuel lines; long enough to interrupt water supplies and disrupt cell, Internet, and phone service.

Imagine what your school or home would look like in the aftermath of such an earthquake: furniture knocked down, the floor a mess of shattered objects mixed with glass shards and plaster and paint dust. In your neighborhood, roads are buckled, houses have slid off their foundations, downed power lines thrash and crackle, and water spurts from broken pipes. Smoke from fires drifts by as car alarms and sirens scream.

If you're on the Pacific Northwest coast, the situation is much worse. Land all along the shore has dropped as much as six feet (almost 2 meters) and the quaking has been more violent. As soon as the shaking stops, you bolt as fast as you can to high ground. The ocean recedes behind you, baring a long expanse of sand and mud. Offshore, the ocean rises up like a dam about to burst. Twenty minutes later, with an ominous gurgling *whoosh,* a series of unstoppable swells, called a tsunami, speeds into shore. The water surges inland, lifting boats, cars, piers, and even buildings with great crunches and crashes.

The current is so powerful that no one can remain standing in even knee-deep water. You watch from a high hill for hours as the roiling, debris-filled water rises and spreads

Murakami Misato surveys the damage done to her bedroom on the fourth floor of an apartment block in Kesennuma, Japan, after a 9.0 magnitude earthquake struck on March 11, 2011.

across roads, yards, playgrounds, and parking lots, scouring the ground again and again. When the tsunami finally recedes, it leaves behind a wasteland.

The Pacific Northwest can be an idyllic place to live, with its endless beaches, lush forests, rolling coastal range, bubbling waterfalls, and glacier-capped volcanic peaks. Temperatures are mild and the region suffers no hurricanes or typhoons, few thunderstorms, and even fewer tornadoes.

And just thirty years ago, no one suspected that a disaster like a mega-earthquake could ever happen there. California, with its massive system of faults, including the

San Andreas, was the place for dangerous earthquakes. Every year Californians are jostled by several hundred earthquakes greater than magnitude 3.0, and fifteen to twenty greater than magnitude 4.0. In the last hundred years, California has suffered forty earthquakes between 6.0 and 6.9 magnitude and sixteen with magnitudes in the sevens.

In contrast, the Pacific Northwest seems remarkably peaceful, with just a handful of small earthquakes causing noticeable shaking each year. In the last hundred years, only a few medium-size quakes have hit near Seattle and Mendocino.

But a few decades ago, scientists discovered a geological structure running along the Pacific Northwest coast that in other parts of the world regularly triggers massive earthquakes—quakes of magnitude 8.0 and higher. Geologists (scientists who study the Earth's structures and processes) also found some odd features they couldn't explain: ghost forests, strange sand layers, and marshes buried below other marshes. Ancient stories from people native to the Pacific Northwest coast—and from far across the Pacific Ocean in Japan—offered more clues that the region might not be as geologically peaceful as it seems.

To solve the puzzle posed by the geology of the Pacific Northwest, a small group of dedicated scientists has been analyzing marsh soil, tracking sediments on the ocean floor, sampling landslide debris, and counting rings in ghost forests. Their findings are transforming our understanding of the region called Cascadia, the grave dangers the population faces, and what can be done to prepare.

This is their story.

THE MEANING OF MAGNITUDE

Scientists express the power and energy released at the source (or epicenter) of an earthquake using a scale from 0 to 10, called the Moment Magnitude Scale. But on this scale, the power does not increase equally step by step. Rather, each step up the scale (from 3.0 to 4.0, for example) indicates an earthquake with thirty-two times more energy released.

A 9.0 magnitude earthquake is *thirty-two thousand times* more powerful than a 6.0, with almost one hundred times more energy released.

A tsunami breeches an embankment and flows into Miyako, Japan, shortly after a 9.0 magnitude earthquake hit the region in March 2011.

The Cascade volcano Mount Rainier, which lies about 60 miles southeast of Seattle.

CHAPTER ONE

THE MYSTERY OF THE MISSING EARTHQUAKES

NOT TOO LONG AGO, when your grandparents were kids, their teachers and textbooks had no explanation for what created mountains. No one knew why some ranges loomed steep and jagged while others lay low, round, and smooth. Geologists had no good ideas about what caused earthquakes. We didn't even know how continents were formed or why some of their coastlines matched like pieces of a jigsaw puzzle.

"Until surprisingly recently, science had no good answers to these very basic questions," says Chris Goldfinger, professor of geology and geophysics at Oregon State University. "I'm talking about up until the 1960s, geologists just had no idea how or why any of these things existed."

More than a hundred years ago, a German weather forecaster named Alfred Wegener took a shot at explaining how continents formed. Scientists had long ago noticed that the coastlines of various continents *looked* like they would fit together. Wegener discovered that the rocks and fossils found on the distant coastlines were, surprisingly, also similar. And the

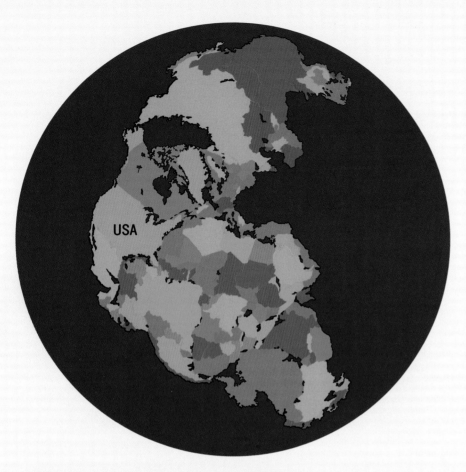

Geologists believe that all Earth's continents originated from one supercontinent called Pangaea. This map shows where the countries of 2012 may have been located on Pangaea.

"Those observations should have rocked every geologist on the planet."

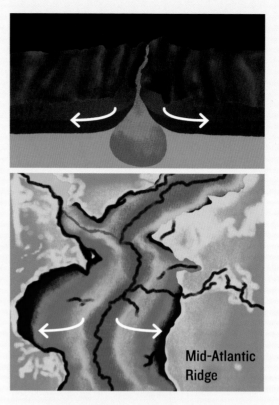

As the tectonic plates beneath the Atlantic Ocean spread, new crust is made from magma rising from below. Scientists discovered this process when they realized that crust was older the farther it was located from the Mid-Atlantic Ridge.

Mid-Atlantic Ridge

grooves scraped into the landscapes by glaciers during the Ice Age seemed to line up from one continent to the other.

Wegener proposed that once, long ago, the Earth had only one big continent that split and drifted apart to become the continents we know today. He called his theory continental drift.

"Those observations should have rocked every geologist on the planet," says Chris. "But that didn't happen. They dismissed him." After all, Wegener was an outsider to geology and he couldn't explain how or why the continents had moved.

So, Wegener's theory was forgotten.

Then, during World War II, submarines scouring the seas for German U-boats found an odd structure on the ocean floor—a ten-thousand-mile-long (16,000 kilometer) ridge running through the Atlantic Ocean from north to south, like a huge zipper. Geologist Marie Tharp mapped

Professor of Geology Chris Goldfinger at Oregon State University in Corvallis.

Marie Tharp with her sea floor maps.

German U-boat U-II8 attacked by aircraft from USS *Bogue*. Planes and ships searching for U-boats helped map the sea floor.

similar ridges in the Pacific Ocean. Over the next few decades, scientists discovered that while rocks on either side of the ridges were old, the rocks near the ridges were newer. Something was creating new sea floor at the ridges and pushing land away on both sides.

"Right about then, Wegener's theory came back to life," says Chris. "People realized, uh-oh, maybe this guy was actually right. Maybe the Earth's crust is moving around."

Geologists quickly embraced a powerful idea that seemed to explain everything: the theory of plate tectonics. According to this now well-established, widely accepted theory, Earth has a crust—a hard shell of rock—that is broken into huge plates. These plates float on a layer of melted rock, drifting slowly apart in some places and bumping into each other in other places.

Plate tectonics explained mountain formation: Plates crash into each other, pushing up the land. Tall, jagged mountain ranges are young; lower, gentler ranges are older and have eroded over time.

Plate tectonics explained earthquakes: As plates slide along each other, sections can get stuck. Pressure builds until that section suddenly gets unstuck, shaking the ground nearby.

And plate tectonics explained really big earthquakes: Plates collide, and the heavier plate pushes under the lighter plate in a process called subduction. Sometimes plates get stuck along the whole zone where the plates meet. The upper plate bows upward, like a yardstick that is being pushed together at both ends. Pressure builds. Finally the top plate releases and everything that was bowed up snaps down, shaking a huge length of land. This rupture causes megaquakes, magnitude 8.0 and up earthquakes that shake for minutes rather than seconds.

Maybe pressure was building all along the Pacific Northwest coast, ready to unleash a megaquake.

But plate tectonics did not explain the Pacific Northwest. About fifty miles (80 kilometers) off the coast, running from British Columbia to Northern California, lies the 620-mile-long (1,000-kilometer) Cascadia Subduction Zone (CSZ), where a heavier plate pushes under a lighter one. Subduction zones circle the Pacific Ocean, creating the Ring of Fire, a geographically active region where 90 percent of the Earth's quakes—and all of the biggest earthquakes—occur.

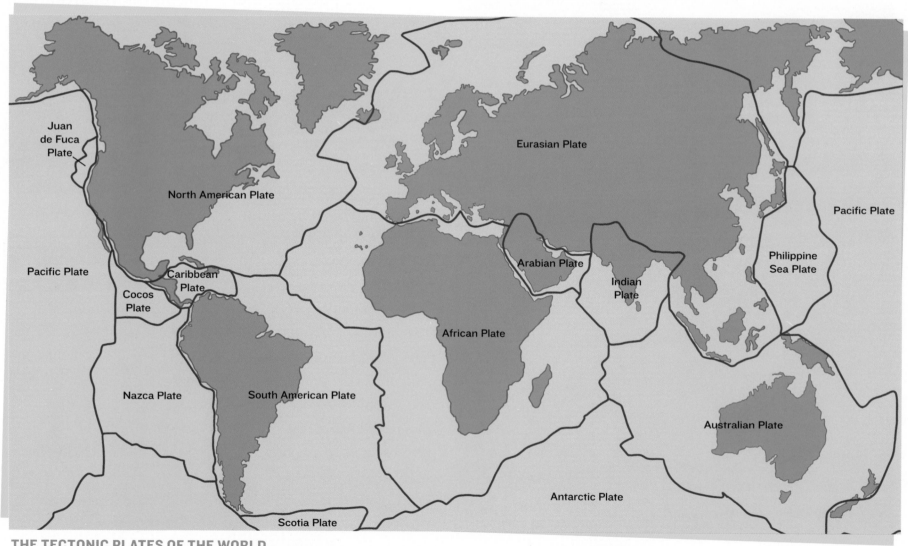

Juan de Fuca Plate

North American Plate

Eurasian Plate

Pacific Plate

Pacific Plate

Caribbean Plate

Cocos Plate

Arabian Plate

Philippine Sea Plate

Indian Plate

African Plate

Nazca Plate

South American Plate

Australian Plate

Antarctic Plate

Scotia Plate

THE TECTONIC PLATES OF THE WORLD

"But Cascadia seemed just dead silent," Chris says. "It was basically the only subduction zone in the world that didn't seem to have earthquakes." There were three possible explanations: Maybe silt, acting like grease on wheels, kept the plates moving steadily. Perhaps the plates had simply stopped moving. Or, most frighteningly, maybe the plates were locked and had been locked for a long time. Maybe pressure was building all along the Pacific Northwest coast, ready to unleash a megaquake.

The lack of massive earthquakes in the Cascadia Subduction Zone was a baffling mystery for scientists. "We've got this great theory, and it fits everything, except it can't explain this," Chris says. "And so Cascadia just sat like a white elephant in the corner and everyone just tippy-toed around it."

For almost forty years.

THE CASCADIA SUBDUCTION ZONE

Much of North America sits on the North American Plate. Just offshore from British Columbia, Washington, Oregon, and Northern California, three smaller, heavier plates—the Juan de Fuca, Explorer, and Gorda Plates—press into the edge of the lighter North American Plate. As the plates slowly collide, the three smaller plates smash beneath the North American Plate, creating the Cascadia Subduction Zone. The inset shows where the CSZ is located on the Ring of Fire.

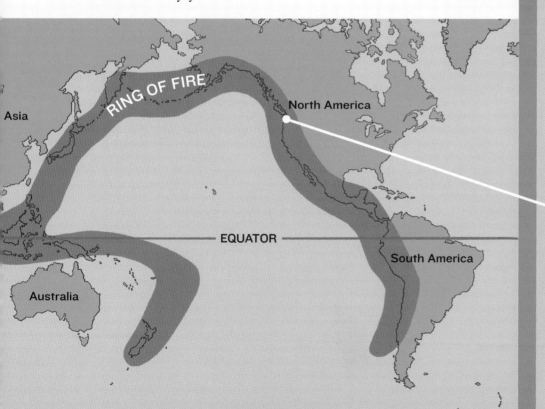

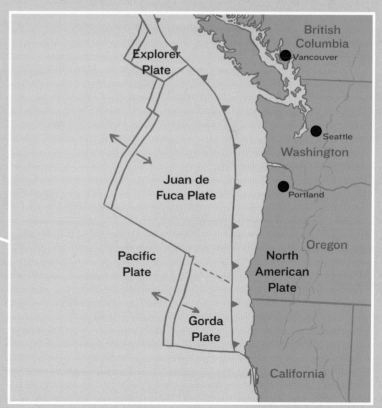

Geologist Brian Atwater (right) boats up the Nestucca River on the Oregon coast with Robert Russell of the Tillamook Bay Watershed Council at the helm.

CHAPTER TWO

SHERLOCK OF THE MARSHES

WHEN BRIAN ATWATER, a geologist for the United States Geological Survey, moved to Seattle in the mid-1980s, he heard that the Pacific Northwest might be due for a huge earthquake—or not. He was surprised that there was little proof either way.

Then, while in the field working on another issue, he discovered something intriguing—evidence that sometime in the past, land along the Washington coast had abruptly dropped in elevation.

Searching for a possible explanation, Brian turned to descriptions of subduction zones in Alaska and Chile. There, as one plate pushed under the other, the top layer slowly bowed up all along the edge. And when the fault ruptured, or slipped, in an earthquake, the bowed land suddenly plunged back down—sometimes dropping as much as eight feet (2.3 meters). The very edge of the plate that had been pushed down also released, snapping up and giving the ocean a shove. Tsunamis swept inland, flooding the lowered land with salty, sandy water.

If the Cascadia Subduction Zone had created huge quakes, Brian reasoned, he should be able to find more evidence of dramatic land drops followed by tsunamis all along the Pacific Northwest coast.

So he set out with a shovel and a World War II–era trenching hoe to explore tidal marshes along coastal rivers and estuaries. "Salt marshes and the plants that live there are very sensitive to changes in conditions, so they are good recorders of land-level changes," he says.

Brian approached each expedition as though he were a detective—he was searching for clues, trying to solve the mystery of whether or not Cascadia had suffered earthquakes. The main clue he sought: a buried marsh where all plant life had suddenly been covered by sand.

SUBDUCTION ZONE QUAKES

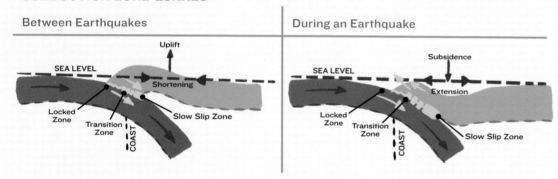

Between Earthquakes

Uplift

SEA LEVEL

Shortening

Locked Zone

Transition Zone

COAST

Slow Slip Zone

During an Earthquake

Subsidence

SEA LEVEL

Extension

Locked Zone

Transition Zone

COAST

Slow Slip Zone

HOW A TSUNAMI BURIES A MARSH

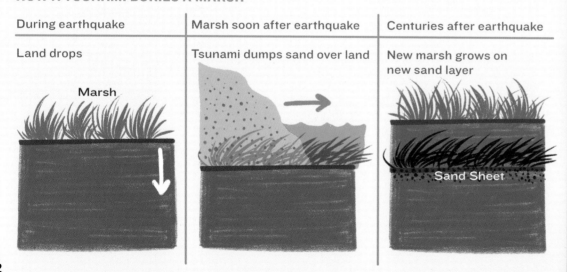

During earthquake

Land drops

Marsh

Marsh soon after earthquake

Tsunami dumps sand over land

Centuries after earthquake

New marsh grows on new sand layer

Sand Sheet

Brian Atwater is puzzled by bluish tinted mud he uncovers on the riverbank. He suspects it is sediment from upriver.

A Clue?

Brian gets up close and personal with the mud as he tries to find a layer of sand possibly laid down by a tsunami.

While Brian often travels by canoe on these excursions, for a recent trip down the Nestucca River in Oregon, he climbs into the front of a metal fishing boat captained by Robert Russell of the Tillamook Bay Watershed Council. Floating downstream and with the outgoing tide, Robert gently rows the boat as gulls scream overhead and herons strut through marsh grass. Brian can't wait to get out of the boat and into the mud.

He spots an exposed bank. "Here," Brian says, and practically tumbles out of the boat as Robert pulls over. Within seconds Brian is hacking away at the wall of a dirt bank exposed by the low tide, bits of mud flying everywhere. Below the tree roots of the marsh plants, he scrapes through a layer of mud, a two-finger-deep layer of sand, then another layer of smooth mud. Could these be clues that the marsh

dropped suddenly and then was buried by sand swept inland by a tsunami? "I can't tell for sure," Brian says. "The sand layer could have been made by a tsunami—or by sand blown from that dune."

Brian climbs back into the boat, scrutinizing the riverbank as they head downstream. "That's nicely striped," he says. He leaps out of the boat as soon as it lodges on a mud shelf. The rush of the constantly changing tides has already carved this bank, but Brian smooths it with his hand tool and kneels down to see more clearly.

The lower layer of mud has a strange bluish tint. "This is mystifying," Brian says. The blue suggests that this layer could be sediment washed down by the river, not the remains of a buried marsh.

Brian splashes into the river and marches knee deep along the river's edge, following the thin bluish line, which soon turns more brown. As the tide gets lower and he heads toward the mouth of the river, more of the riverbank is exposed. Here, some of the layers are hollowed out. Brian suspects these are areas where water has washed away layers of sand. He chops into the wall, hauling hunks of mud out of the way, until he reaches the missing layer—it is sand.

"Now how can I be sure that this sand was laid down hundreds of years ago by a tsunami?" Like a sleuth scouring a crime scene, Brian picks through the mud and sand. He's hoping to find something dead—remnants of marsh plants. He'd be happy with a plant fossil in the layer of mud—or even better, a plant sticking up from the mud into the sand. "That would mean that the plant literally died standing up, when the ground suddenly dropped and sand swept in," he says. He pokes and prods and crumbles material through his fingers, but finds nothing.

Brian continues like this, boating and tromping downstream, trying to follow the layers as he goes, hacking off pieces of the marsh, carving out the layers below, and even lying down in the mud to peer at the layers. Though it's June, the weather is typical for the Pacific Northwest coast: gray, cold, and rainy. But Brian is oblivious to the cold, to the wet, and even to the muck coating his coveralls and splattering his face. He is determined to find and read clues that will tell him definitively that sometime in the past, the land here dropped and was covered by a tsunami and eventually another marsh.

Finally, as he's chopping into a bank, he exclaims: "Ohhh!" He scrapes off a wider expanse of mud just below a sand layer. He grins. "Do you see the smile?" he asks. He's

Brian Atwater considers whether the dune across the river could be the source of sand buried in the riverbank.

The riverbank is riddled with underwater root systems from large plants and trees that were once above ground—before the coast dropped several feet in elevation from a Cascadia quake.

A Clue?

The treasures Brian searches for in the mud are plants buried upright in a sandy layer below the marsh mud. They signify that the plants were suddenly buried in sand while standing up, something that could only happen in a tsunami. Brian discovers the V-shape roots of seaside arrowgrass in the brown sand. Living seaside arrowgrass can also be found in the marsh above the mud and sand. This is all conclusive evidence of a massive subduction zone earthquake and tsunami.

not referring to the one on his face. There in the mud, a brownish, pencil-thin, broad smile stretches across in the gray mud. It's a plant fossil, the distinctive remnant of the salt marsh plant *Triglochin maritima,* also known as seaside arrowgrass. A fist-size layer of sand lies above it.

Brian is buoyant: "This is as good as it gets for hard evidence of a subduction zone quake and tsunami." He and others have spent years paddling and wading up rivers and through marshes and estuaries all along the Pacific Northwest coast—and have uncovered a clear record of a huge subduction zone earthquake. "It has taken so much intensive field work," he says. "Not at just a few sites, but at hundreds of sites."

Brian is still not ready to turn back. The more evidence he can gather, the more he will know about what happened here. Just a little farther downstream, while hacking into mud from the sunken marsh, he hits something hard—rock hard. "Now how did a rock get buried in here?" Brian surveys the scene: the high bank of sand and modern marsh, a cluster of spruce trees, and the rippling water stirred up by Chinook salmon sweeping by. And as he has noticed all along the trip, there are no other rocks around.

The scientist-detective puts all the clues together. "Tides and rivers move silt and clay, wind and tsunamis move sand, but only one thing could have moved a rock to this old marsh," he says. "Humans." Sometime long ago, before the coast was clobbered by a megaquake that dropped the land more than five feet (1.5 meters) and then was covered with heaps of sand from a tsunami, this spot might have been a native fishing camp.

And stories of the people who once lived and fished here might offer clues about when this catastrophe last struck.

Puget Sound on the Pacific Coast by American landscape painter Albert Bierstadt.

CHAPTER THREE

CLUES FROM THE PAST

HUNDREDS OF THOUSANDS of native people lived in nations all along the Pacific Northwest for thousands of years before the Oregon Trail brought waves of settlers to the West Coast.

While the immigrants of the 1800s never reported a Cascadia earthquake, geologists realized that native people may have. In the 1990s, Ruth Ludwin, an earthquake scientist at the University of Washington, began searching for oral history accounts of shaking and marine flooding up and down the Pacific Northwest. And she found them.

A member of the Cowichan tribe of British Columbia recounted: "In the days before the white man, there was a great earthquake. It began about the middle of one night. [It] brought great masses of rock down from the mountain. One village was completely buried beneath a landslide. It was a very terrible experience; the people could neither stand nor sit for the extreme motion of the earth."

People had heard about a destructive tsunami as well. "There was a big flood shortly before the white man's time," Susan Ned of the Coquille Indian Tribe of Coos Bay told her granddaughter. "A huge tidal wave that struck the Oregon coast not too far back in time . . .

the ocean rose up and huge waves swept and surged across the land. Trees were uprooted and villages were swept away."

Chief Louis Nookmis described a similar disaster that destroyed a coastal village on Vancouver Island: "They had practically no way or time to try and save themselves . . . it was nighttime that the land shook . . . a big wave smashed into the beach. The Pachena Bay people were lost. But those who lived at . . . House-Up-Against-Hill, the wave did not reach because they were on high ground . . . Because of that they came out alive. They did not drift out to sea with the others."

Ruth and her colleagues scrutinized the stories for details that would suggest when the disasters happened. They estimated that a large earthquake and tsunami struck the Pacific Northwest sometime between 1690 and 1715. This estimate matched radiocarbon dating of twigs and other plant material from the buried marshes along the coast.

Would they be able to figure out exactly when this earthquake occurred?

〰〰〰

In 1995, Brian Atwater read a draft of an article by Kenji Satake of the Geological Survey of Japan describing accounts written by samurai, merchants, and peasants in coastal Japan of a mysterious tsunami. Indeed, a Cascadia Subduction Zone tsunami would not only devastate the Pacific Northwest coast; the surge of water would also head thousands of miles across the Pacific Ocean to Asia.

Atwater was so intrigued that he spent a year with Kenji in Japan exploring this connection. "I often joked that Brian did not believe me, so he came to Japan for inspection," Kenji says.

In 1700, a town official noted: "Within Kuwagasaki village . . . tsunami came. Villagers escaped to hills. Thirteen houses destroyed by waves . . . Housing lost, temporary shelter wanted."

The leader of the Miho village gave this detailed account: "High tide or something entered . . . reached up the pine groves . . . seven times rose. To the old, the wave's appearance was unusual . . . the whole village was puzzled . . . Could it be tsunami? For many years we must remember it well . . . Earthquake did not happen. Only strong waves. Future should keep in mind."

The Japanese kept meticulous records including exact dates and times. This strange orphan tsunami—a tsunami with no preceding earthquake felt in Japan—hit along a whole stretch of Japan's east coast. The Cascadia Subduction Zone was a logical culprit. It fit all the evidence: the sunken

Trembling lasted at least five long minutes, shaking people awake, throwing their possessions to the ground, damaging their houses, and triggering massive landslides.

大海嘯極惨状之圖

A print illustrating the Meiji Sanriku tsunami triggered by a 7.2 magnitude earthquake in Sanriku, Japan, in 1896.

marshes, the ancient tales of shaking and flooding from local Pacific Northwest tribes, and now these accounts of an earthquake-less tsunami striking five thousand miles (8,000 kilometers) away.

Kenji and his colleagues calculated that for a tsunami to reach Japan at midnight of January 27, 1700, from North America, an earthquake of roughly magnitude 9.0 must have shaken the Pacific Northwest. The shaking from such an earthquake would have traveled at jetliner speeds (500 miles/800 kilometers per hour) for ten hours across the Pacific Ocean. That pinpointed the date and time of the most recent Cascadia mega-earthquake at January 26, 1700, at nine p.m.

Scientists were now convinced that on a cold winter night, the bowed North American Plate of the Cascadia

This woodblock print, *Choshi in Soshu Province* from *A Thousand Pictures of the Sea* (c. 1833) by Hokusai, depicts a giant ocean wave receding from the Japanese coast.

20

JAPAN

CANADA

UNITED STATES

How the 1700 Cascadia quake waves moved toward Japan.

Subduction Zone released, dropping land along the coast about five feet (1.5 meters). Trembling lasted at least five long minutes, shaking people awake, throwing their possessions to the ground, damaging their houses, and triggering massive landslides. A tsunami blasted two coasts, wiping away whole villages while the survivors staggered to high ground.

But that is not the end of the Cascadia story. If Cascadia has had one mega-earthquake, could it unleash another?

Thousands of people lived in the Pacific Northwest during the horrific 1700 earthquake. Today roughly *seven million* people and their buildings, roads, bridges, schools, and hospitals sit squarely in the danger zone.

Scientists had to try to figure out when the next big one might strike.

Could it be in our lifetimes?

The research vessel *Thompson*, which carried
Chris Goldfinger and his team to sea.

CHAPTER FOUR

A PREPOSTEROUS THEORY

TO BEGIN FIGURING OUT when the next Cascadia earthquake might strike, geologists needed to find out how frequently the subduction zone had ruptured before. Back in 1985, John Adams, a scientist with the Geological Survey of Canada, thought there might be clues buried in the ocean floor. He thought he might find evidence of ancient landslides triggered by Cascadia earthquakes in the layers of mud. So he examined descriptions of ocean-soil core samples taken in the 1960s.

John found one layer in each core that was easily explained: a layer of volcanic ash from Mount Mazama's eruption 7,600 years ago, which formed Oregon's Crater Lake. When he counted debris layers, called turbidites, he noticed an interesting pattern. The Mazama ash was always the thirteenth layer down from the top. He observed this in sample after sample.

John thought it was unlikely that this was a coincidence. If the debris layers were caused by local storms, regional earthquakes, or the small eruptions of nearby volcanoes,

CAN I GO WITH YOU GUYS?

Chris Goldfinger has been fascinated by science since he was about six years old, when he got a geology book as a gift. "It was full of exploding volcanoes and earthquakes," he remembers. "Full of action you could see without a microscope."

An experience walking down the hallway peering into all the science classrooms in high school cemented his interest in geology. "There were all the chemistry people with their little glasses and white coats making funny-colored liquids, and the biologists were in the same outfits picking frogs apart, and the geology class was loading up the station wagon with a cooler to go to the mountains," he recalls. "I was like, 'Can I go with you guys?'"

Geologist Chris Goldfinger studies a soil core from the bottom of the Pacific Ocean, searching for layers of debris, called turbidites, in the sample.

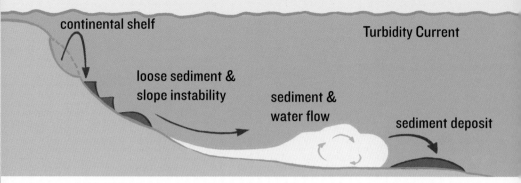

How earthquakes deposit sediment on the ocean floor.

they would only show up in the ocean near where the event happened. He would not have seen evidence of exactly the same number of events along the coasts of both Oregon and Washington. His theory: The debris layers were formed by thirteen massive earthquakes over the last 7,600 years—thirteen subduction zone earthquakes.

"I thought John's theory was preposterous," says Chris Goldfinger. Chris was sure that if more cores were taken from more places and studied more closely with modern technology, they would find cores that did not match the thirteen-layer pattern. So Chris and colleague Hans Nelson set out to prove John Adams wrong.

In 1999, Chris and Hans and nine geology students loaded up a three-hundred-foot-long (90 meter) research vessel called *Melville*. "Going out on an oceanographic cruise is like going out to sea in a small floating factory, chugging black diesel smoke," says Chris. He laughs and quotes Samuel Johnson: "It's like jail with the additional possibility of drowning."

It was a strange voyage, Chris remembers. At first many of the team members were seasick. "Plus, it was kind of weird that we going out to *dis*prove a hypothesis," he says. "Usually you're working to prove a hypothesis."

The ocean floor coring team prepares to lower the coring device into the ocean. It will be turned 90 degrees to point downward and then dropped into the muddy floor.

"Going out on an oceanographic cruise is like . . . jail with the additional possibility of drowning."

To collect core samples of the ocean floor, the ship cruised to a target spot, usually over a canyon where sediments collected. The team placed the coring device horizontally onto a crane. With a call of "Ready!" the crane driver lifted the instrument over the water, rotated it until it looked like a downward-facing rocket, and began to lower it ten thousand feet (3,000 meters) to the ocean floor. The force of gravity then pushed the coring device's tube twenty-five to thirty feet (8 to 10 meters) deep into the mud.

A piston at the top of the device held the sediments in place inside the tube, like a finger closing the top of a straw, as the winch slowly pulled the device back up through the water. Wind and waves jostled the ship as the team guided the long steel pipe back on the deck. The whole process of grabbing one core took three or four hours.

And that was just the beginning.

The team sliced the long core into five-foot (1.5 meter) sections and carried them below deck, into a lab. There, graduate students ran the sections through an instrument that mapped the hardness, density, magnetism, and resistance to electricity of the layers in the sample. Then the students slid a stiff wire, like a cheese cutter, lengthwise through the middle of the core, cutting it in half. When they banged it on the table, the core fell open like a book.

They immediately snapped high-resolution photos of the mud. Then, perched on stools, hovering over the mud like coroners over a body, the students wrote millimeter-by-millimeter descriptions of the layers in the core: What color was each layer? Did the soil seem sandy, muddy, or claylike? How fine or rough were the grains?

Halfway through the trip, Chris and Hans had a chance to look at what they had collected so far. The pair hauled a bunch of cores out onto the deck and laid them out side by side. Then they bent down to take a close look.

"Oh!" Chris exclaimed, almost immediately.

There it was, as clear as day. The cores all had thirteen debris layers above the Mazama ash.

Sample after sample had proven John Adams's preposterous theory.

Chris immediately sent John an email saying: "Looks like you were right." The evidence was clear and unmistakable.

Underwater landslides had been triggered exactly thirteen times at the same time intervals all along the whole Cascadia Subduction Zone. Local events like storms, earthquakes, or small volcanic eruptions would not reach far enough to churn up soil all along the 620-mile (1,000-kilometer) coast. Only a powerful, widespread event such as a Cascadia Subduction Zone earthquake could have done that.

"Right then I became a paleoseismologist," says Chris. (Paleoseismologists study rocks and sediments for evidence of ancient earthquakes.) "I've been doing it ever since and so has Hans."

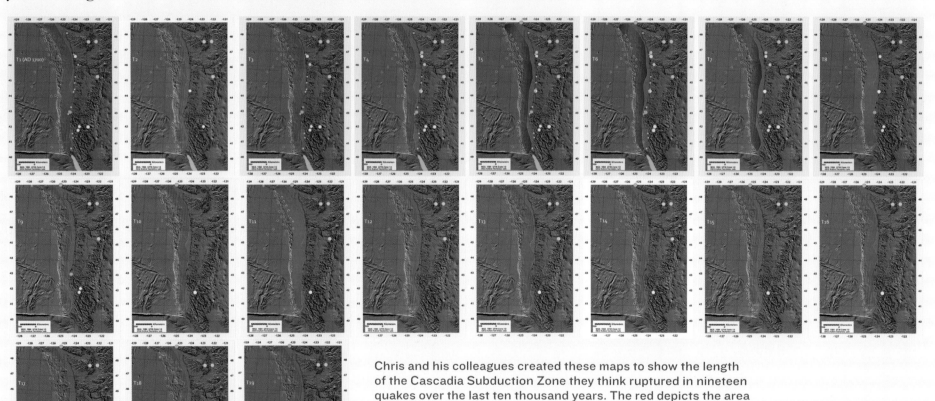

Chris and his colleagues created these maps to show the length of the Cascadia Subduction Zone they think ruptured in nineteen quakes over the last ten thousand years. The red depicts the area of the fault that ruptured. The dots show locations where the scientists gathered data used to make the map.

Jim Schmid and Ann Morey mark the core liner in preparation for cutting the core into sections and splitting them in half for onboard analysis.

In three more cruises, in 2002, 2009, and 2015, Chris and his team gathered several hundred more ocean floor cores. They found evidence of an astounding *forty-six* large events in the last ten thousand years. Some involved only part of the fault, usually the southern section. But nineteen quakes seemed to have ruptured the full length of the subduction zone from British Columbia to Mendocino, California. These were the big ones, the 9.0s. "We went from thinking this area had no earthquakes to thinking 'Uh-oh.'"

Given how regularly Cascadia seems to rupture, a mega-earthquake—an earthquake bigger than one ever seen near the San Andreas—is a certainty. "The question is not whether an 8.0 or higher Cascadia earthquake could happen," says Chris. "It *will* happen."

To estimate *when* the next big one might strike, Chris and his colleagues analyzed the lapsed time between earthquakes. They put the odds of a mega-earthquake hitting British Columbia and Washington sometime in the next fifty years at 10 to 17 percent. They posit the chances of one striking Oregon in that same time frame are 15 to 20 percent. And the danger of a subduction zone earthquake clobbering southern Oregon and Northern California? Thirty-seven percent—or one in three.

But how violent will the shaking really be?

WHAT ARE THE ODDS?

While Chris and his colleagues extracted and analyzed offshore core samples, coastal research like the work conducted by Brian Atwater along the Nestucca River continued. By studying buried marshes and sand sheets spread by tsunamis, taking soil-core and tree-ring samples, and carbon-dating buried material, geologists have constructed an onshore record of Cascadia earthquakes and tsunamis dating back five thousand years.

The consensus based on both onshore and offshore research is that Cascadia ruptures regularly with periods of silence lasting longer than human life spans. But the different research approaches have generated different odds. Onshore research puts the odds of a Cascadia quake striking southern Oregon and Northern California in the next fifty years as much lower—one in ten.

Different results aren't too surprising given that soil moves and is preserved differently on land and under the ocean and that the researchers are studying evidence of different phenomena triggered by subduction zone earthquakes—dropping of elevation along the coast and tsunami sand deposits versus mud moving great distances underwater. "Discrepancies and disagreements are healthy in science," Brian says. "They help fuel scientific advances."

University of Washington graduate student Susie Wisehart leads a team of researchers into a dense forest toward a pond formed by a landslide. They carry the parts they need to build a raft to float on the pond.

CHAPTER FIVE
LESSONS FROM LANDSLIDES

WHEN A CASCADIA EARTHQUAKE STRIKES, it will not shake the whole Pacific Northwest evenly. Trembling will be more violent close to where the quake starts, along the subduction zone, and at the coast, which is just fifty miles (80 kilometers) from the zone. The shaking will dissipate as the quake reaches the inland valley. But how much movement will rock the I-5 corridor where millions of people live in Portland, Seattle, and other cities and towns?

To find out, teams of scientists have begun to intensely study landslides to figure out which ones may have been triggered by Cascadia quakes. Many slopes are not likely to slide unless shaking is severe, so by identifying Cascadia landslides, researchers can get a picture of how far strong shaking might reach.

The challenge is accurately dating landslides to find the ones that match the dates of Cascadia earthquakes. Scientists are still exploring what method—or combination of methods—is the easiest, most fruitful, and accurate.

Western Washington University graduate student Geoff Malick (left), University of Washington graduate student Susie Wisehart (center), and WWU associate professor Douglas Clark (right) paddle out to a pond formed by the Rowan landslide in Washington State.

The team climbs aboard the raft, pushes off—and goes nowhere.

The Rowan landslide outside Oso, Washington, is a perfect example. Alison Duvall, a principal investigator for the University of Washington's M9 project (which is focused on preparing for a Cascadia earthquake) and graduate students Susie Wisehart and Sean LaHusen are attacking the problem a number of different ways. Sean has hiked in gullies and to terraces cut into the Rowan slide and collected six little bits of preserved wood from the debris. Carbon dating put their ages anywhere from three hundred to almost seven hundred years old.

Susie wants to compare those dates to dates calculated from woody material taken from nearby Rowan slide debris at the bottom of a pond. "Ponds that formed when the landslide occurred may hold woody debris we can use to date the landslide," she says.

To take the soil cores, the team gathers at a gated dirt road. They hike all their gear off-trail through a dense forest to their research site. After an hour, they arrive at the football-field-size circle of dark water surrounded by leafing and evergreen trees and half-covered in tan-colored peat. Lily pads float on the dark water and frogs ribbit and croak.

Their first task is to assemble their raft. Susie hacks at some blackberries with her machete to clear a work area. With foot pumps, Douglas Clark, an associate professor at Western Washington University who has hauled his makeshift research raft into dozens of lakes, inflates two canoes and builds a wooden deck between them. This takes another hour.

"Ready . . . LIFT," says Doug, and the team inches its way down toward the dark water where they lower the raft's nose into the water. The team climbs aboard the raft, pushes off— and goes nowhere. Susie paddles, Doug poles, and they still don't budge. Finally Doug hops into the water and lifts the heavy raft as much as he can until it dislodges from behind a stump. Slowly they glide out into the pond, poling from the back of the raft and paddling from the front, like adults playing Huck Finn.

The soil-coring process is similar to Chris Goldfinger's ocean coring. Only without a crane, they do everything by hand. It's slow going. After securing the raft in the center of the pond, Doug and Susie guide the coring pipe through a hole in the deck, into the water and to the pond bottom. They begin to push and twist. After only about eight inches (20 centimeters), they stop. They've hit a log that probably toppled long after the slide.

The team hauls the core back up and repositions the raft over a different spot on the pond. When they push the coring pipe into the pond bottom, it slides in easily. "That's better," Doug says. "This is what a good fluffy lake bed should do."

Alison Duvall, a principal investigator for the University of Washington's M9 project, examines mud that ran out of the coring pipe and checks for woody pieces. She and the other researchers also take detailed notes in field notebooks.

HOW OLD IS OLD?

Scientists in many fields use a technique called carbon dating to determine the age of something that was once alive. Everything alive on Earth absorbs an element called carbon. Carbon consists of 99 percent carbon-12, a little less than 1 percent carbon-13, and even less radioactive carbon-14.

When something such as a tree branch dies, it stops absorbing carbon. The amount of carbon-12 in the branch will remain about the same forever. But radioactive carbon, carbon-14, in the branch will immediately start to decay.

In fact, carbon-14 decays at a steady rate that scientists know well. The amount of carbon-14 will drop by half about every 5,730 years. (Scientists say that carbon-14 has a half-life of 5,730 years.)

To date an old piece of wood, scientists measure the amount of carbon-14 and carbon-12 in the sample. They compare those amounts and calculate what percentage of the carbon-14 remains. If 50 percent of the original carbon-14 remains, the piece of wood from the tree branch is about 5,730 years old. If only a quarter remains, it is about 11,460 years, and so on.

This ingenious method of dating wood, fossils, and other old remains won its creator, Willard Libby, a Nobel Prize in Chemistry in 1960.

Success! When this chunk of soil core breaks off and falls on the raft deck, it reveals a small twig—the woody sample that will help the researchers date the landslide that formed this pond.

The scientists pull up the three-foot-long (1 meter) core. But the sample is not solid; rather, it's a runny, mucky mess. They try a third time, pushing three feet deeper—only to pull up more runny mud that slops all over the deck. The team gives a collective "Ugh."

The sun is getting lower on the horizon, they still have to disassemble the raft and hike out, and the team doesn't have a usable core yet. They decide to try one last time, pushing almost ten feet (3 meters) into the bottom of the pond.

Doug starts narrating as soon as he hits soil: "Okay, we're there. I still feel some grit, it's the same stuff. But there is stiffness now, definitely more stiffness." He strains to push the pipe in deeper. "This is a good sign," he grunts. He forces the coring device as deep as possible to make sure it's in the landslide debris.

Then Doug and Susie slide the sample out. It seems thicker, more solid, like sand mixed in clay. Susie grabs tape

Susie celebrates a good day's work: two soil cores to analyze in the lab.

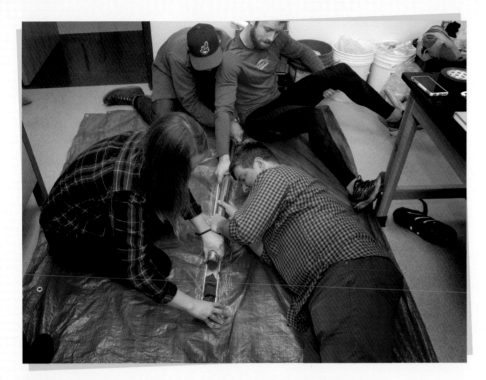

Back at the lab, extracting soil from the pond cores takes many hands and maneuvers, like a game of Twister.

Susie uses a microscope and tweezers to extricate pieces of woody debris for carbon dating.

and wraps the bottom and top to hold the core in.

But as Doug lifts the core to move it to a safer place on the raft, the tape at the bottom slips off. "Oh, oh, OH!" Doug cries. They all dive to try to catch the sample before it slides out of its tube. But a four-inch (10 centimeter) chunk does fall, landing on the edge of the raft. Doug cups it in his hands and picks it up gingerly, as though it's a delicate piece of china.

Then Susie laughs and points at a small twig sticking out of the landslide soil in his hands.

"YES!" Alison hoots. "This is fantastic!" A perfect piece of organic material to send to the lab for carbon dating.

Susie grins. "Looks like we got what we came for."

When the team receives the carbon-dating results from the lab, they're inconclusive. It dates the Rowan slide anywhere from 91 to 358 years ago. Susie's upper range of dates overlaps with Sean's lower range. "I think this method is great for establishing the minimum age of a slide," Susie says.

But there is no telling if Rowan was triggered by a Cascadia quake—or not. The scientists are not discouraged. "When I find myself excited or disappointed with a finding, I remind myself that it is just data," says Alison. "It's just information that will get us closer to the truth."

Hundreds of miles to the south from where Alison's team works, Josh Roering, professor of earth sciences at the University of Oregon in Eugene, and PhD candidate Will Struble are exploring a more precise method of dating landslides, a method that can give the exact year of a slide rather than a wide range. But it requires a very specific, hard-to-find setting: a ghost forest.

Research sawyer Jay Sexton at Klickitat Lake, Oregon, which was formed when a landslide dammed a creek.

For their scientific adventure, they drive deep into the mountain range that runs along the Oregon coast. They weave down bumpy, winding roads rutted with potholes and puddles, and pull up next to sparking blue-green Klickitat Lake. Rising up from the lake are stubby stumps of standing dead trees called snags, with brown, rotted tops that come to crooked coned points, like Hogwarts sorting hats.

This ghost forest was formed when a landslide dropped heaps of soil and rock, damming creeks and streams. Water welled up behind the dam, creating a lake. When the water cut off oxygen to the trees' roots, they died standing upright.

Josh, Will, and research sawyer Jay Sexton are here to find out exactly what year the trees died by counting tree rings. Every year, a tree's growth shows up as a distinct ring inside its trunk. Cutting a wedge from the dead tree reveals these rings without destroying the snag.

Jay quietly unpacks his equipment. He climbs into chest-high waders and dons goggles, an orange helmet, and ear plugs.

The lake is quiet and smells slightly of skunk cabbage and leaf rot. Birds flit from tree to tree chirping, and the water gently laps at the shore.

Then, *putter, putter, rum, RUMMMMMMM!* Jay cranks up his chainsaw.

He steps into the water, his feet sinking into the mud, and leans in toward one of the ghost trees. The chainsaw hits the trunk with a shrill buzz. *Tszzzzzz,* he pushes the rounded tip in. *Tszzzzzzz,* he pulls it out. Again and again, he moves the

Josh Roering, professor of earth sciences at the University of Oregon, protects his ears from the roar of the chainsaw.

Research sawyer Jay Sexton.

Jay pulls the wedge of wood that he carved out of a dead tree on Klickitat Lake.

PhD candidate Will Struble counts tree rings to get a first estimate of the age of a dead tree. Lab analysis will help pinpoint when the tree died, which will give a date for the landslide that trapped the water that killed the tree.

saw ever deeper into the trunk, sawdust flying as he carves out a chunk from the side of the tree.

Peace reigns again when Jay finishes and turns off the saw. He pries the wedge from the trunk and hands it to Will and Josh.

Josh rubs the sawdust away and studies the rings. "This is beautiful."

The pair hope to harvest three to five wedges from a dozen ghost forests all around Oregon. Which ones, they wonder, were formed by a 1700 quake?

To find what Will and Josh call the "Death Ring," from the last year the tree was alive, they will dry the slab with fans for a few days, sand it smooth, and photograph it. They count the rings, measure the ring widths digitally, and email the data off to Bryan Black, a dendrochronologist (a scientist who counts tree rings) from the University of Arizona. Bryan is skilled at finding reference years—such as a period of severe drought—by examining the widths of tree rings. Counting rings outward from these reference years to the bark pinpoints exactly the year the tree died.

But Will, Josh, and Jay can't wait to check out the rings themselves. Will kneels down next to the rough sample and begins counting rings using the tip of his pen to focus his eyes.

Josh watches closely until he gets to the end. "The moment of truth," he says.

"Two hundred thirty-seven-ish," Will announces. The "ish" is the margin of uncertainty. The tightly packed tree rings of varying width are hard to distinguish on a rough cut with the naked eye. Still, the researchers bet each other on when the tree died. Will says 1770, Jay guesses 1757, and Josh pegs it at 1752.

HOW HARD WILL IT SHAKE?

Scientists are working hard to add more detail to this very rough hazard map that estimates the shaking that people in different areas of the country might face from earthquakes. The deep red along the Pacific Northwest coast captures the shaking hazard created by the Cascadia Subduction Zone.

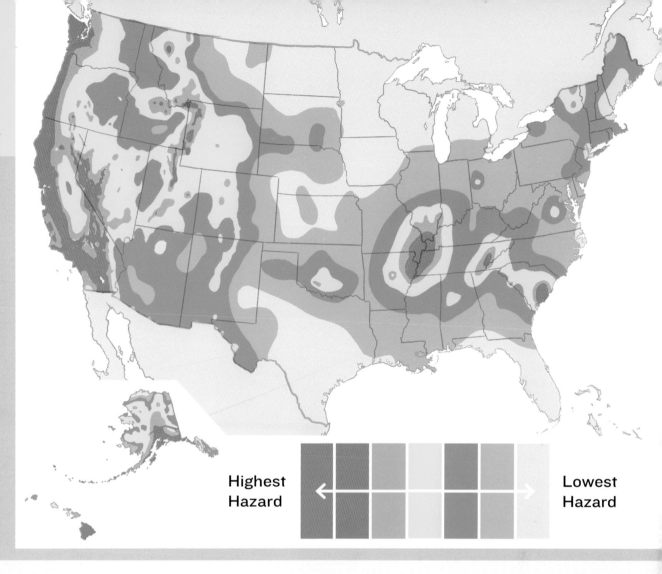

Highest Hazard ← → Lowest Hazard

None of these dates match the 1700 Cascadia quake. That's why the team is not surprised when the tree-ring specialist comes to the conclusion that the trees died in the winter of 1751–52. (Josh wins the bet.) While this landslide was not triggered by a Cascadia quake, Josh and Will know that this technique can help them find landslides that were.

"Currently no one can point a finger to an actual landslide in the coast range linked to 1700," says Josh. "It will be exciting if we do." Finding Cascadia-trigger landslides will be an important step toward understanding how ground shaking spreads from the subduction zone through the coast range to population centers.

And that information will be welcomed by the engineers designing structures such as bridges and buildings to survive a megaquake.

Cereal boxes toppled off the shelves of Miller's Market in Mineral, Virginia, after a 5.8 magnitude earthquake.

CHAPTER SIX
AN OUNCE OF PREVENTION

ON MARCH 11, 2011, at 2:48 p.m. Chris Goldfinger and forty other geologists were gathered in a second-floor conference room in Kashiwa, Japan, discussing the 2004 Sumatra earthquake, when the building began to tremble. Their first reaction? They laughed. *Having an earthquake during an earthquake meeting,* Chris thought. *How funny is that?*

As the shaking continued and the blinds started slapping against the windows, the scientists considered their options. "I looked at these little plastic tables and I thought, there's no need to get under that, that's not going to be very helpful," Chris says. So they grabbed their jackets and headed down the stairs and outside to an open courtyard.

Higher up in the building, where the swaying was stronger, computer monitors slid to the floor and people stumbled as they evacuated. A flagpole on top of the building whipped back and forth. But no one got hurt. "So the first thing I learned is that subduction zone earthquakes don't actually shake that hard," says Chris.

Chris Higgins, professor of civil and construction engineering at Oregon State University and director of OSU's Structural Engineering Research Lab (left), prepares to test bridge columns with PhD candidate Sharoo Shrestha (right).

Engineers in Oregon State University's structural lab check for cracking on a column built to mimic bridge columns common in Oregon.

But they do shake for a long time. While a typical quake may last ten to thirty seconds, a subduction zone quake lasts several minutes. When the trembling first started, the scientists checked their watches. "We're going: 'How long? It's like three minutes; okay, now four minutes and it hasn't stopped yet.' It seemed like a lifetime." Still, Chris didn't fear for his own safety. "We were in Japan with very well-engineered buildings. Things don't fall down in Japan during an earthquake." That's because Japan has been dealing with and building for large earthquakes for hundreds of years.

"People hear about the Cascadia earthquake and they go, 'Oh my god, we're all going to die,'" says Chris. "But that is not the only option. The other path is the Japanese way." The Japanese way is building and retrofitting structures to withstand massive quakes.

Engineers with the Cascadia Lifelines Program have been conducting research to find the best ways to do just that. An ordinary-looking concrete column stands ready for testing in Oregon State University's Structural Engineering Research Laboratory. Square, light gray, with a wide base, and standing eight feet (2.4 meters) high, the column looks like the bottom half of any bridge column in the Pacific Northwest. That's no accident. Sharoo Shrestha, a graduate student working on her PhD in structural engineering, built the column from scratch, following typical Oregon bridge design. She even used a special recipe from the 1950s called "OSU Old Fashioned Concrete."

In a state where most bridges were built before any awareness of the threat posed by Cascadia earthquakes, columns were designed to withstand only two forces: gravity (the weight of the structure and trucks) and wind. "An earthquake is like the Jolly Green Giant leaning hard on a structure, trying to push it over, stressing it laterally," says Chris Higgins, professor of civil and construction engineering at OSU and director of the lab. So what exactly would happen, Sharoo and Chris ask, if one of those columns were to be shaken back and forth? And how could the column be retrofitted to survive?

Strength is one key to surviving an earthquake. But perhaps more important is flexibility. Can the structure bend with the shaking and spring back to its original shape? If the supporting metal bars inside don't bounce back, they lose their ability to hold up the structure's weight.

To test how the column might perform in a Cascadia quake, the team attached a machine to the top of the column, which will push and pull the column to slowly shake it back and forth, back and forth.

The researchers think the column will yield (break) when it is displaced (moved) a mere 0.4 inch (10 millimeters). That is less than half an inch—maybe the width of your pinky nail. But cracking could begin much sooner.

Chris dials up the first push on the column—a tiny 0.1 inch (2.5 millimeters). He directs the machine to return the column to its upright position and then pulls it 0.1 inch. He repeats this cycle three times. The movements are invisible to the naked eye.

The team circles around the column, leaning in, searching the column for cracks. There are only tiny white hairline fractures that were there before the test began. "Those are shrinkage cracks that happen as concrete dries," Sharoo explains.

For the next step, Chris doubles the distance the column will be pushed and pulled to 0.2 inch. Thin, gray hairline cracks appear and the team marks them with pink pens.

Chris moves the column 0.3 inch (7.6 millimeters) back

Sharoo marks tiny cracks on the column that has been retrofitted with titanium coils (the horizontal stripes) around the part of the column with the fragile rebar splice.

and forth, back and forth. "We can see the cracks much better now," Sharoo observes. That's because the cracks are wider. "Wide cracks are bad because water can get in and deteriorate the structure over time due to corrosion," says Chris.

Before pushing the column to 0.4 inch (10 millimeters), the team pauses to take photos. They want to record exactly what the column looks like before it fails. And they turn on a video camera. That way they can replay what happens.

"Ready to power up?" Chris asks.

"Yes," Sharoo answers.

Chris runs through the push-pull cycles and the team swarms, marking new and longer cracks with green markers. The column resembles a giant map now with roads and rivers and streams designated in different colors. But one pattern stands out. Up until now, most of the cracks have been horizontal. Now a number of long diagonal cracks have erupted. These shear cracks indicate weakening from side-to-side movement—a clue that the column may be nearing failure.

But the shear cracks aren't the team's biggest worry. They're really concerned about the reinforcing steel rods (rebar) inside. Most bridges in Oregon were built with a fatal flaw. Instead of long lengths of rebar anchored in the base and running the length of the column, two pieces of rebar are lined up close and tied, or spliced, together. Once the splice fails, the bridge can no longer hold its own weight.

"See how the cracks are clustering here," Sharoo says. She points to an area densely spider-webbed with cracks. "The splice is right here. This is where the column is going to fail."

Chris pushes the column 0.6 inch (15 millimeters)—over a half an inch. A hush falls over the team.

The column begins to crackle and pop. Everyone leans forward, straining to hear. The column pings and crackles and crunches. A dime-size piece of concrete tumbles off.

"Now the other direction," says Chris.

The column clicks and creaks. Cracks rip across the concrete. More chunks fall off.

"Oh wow," someone breathes.

Diagonal cracks erupt all over and form a plate-size piece. "That whole section is ready to break off," someone else says.

Chris allows the column to return upright and the team circles the crumbling column.

"It's done," says Chris. Sharoo, who has been watching the column wide-eyed, confirms it. "If this was an earthquake, the bridge would have buckled under its own weight, falling in that direction," she says.

Failure, as expected, happened between 0.4 and 0.6 inch (10 and 15 millimeters). "It's hard to say what this means

SKYSCRAPERS MADE OF WOOD

Since the Horyu-Ji temple was built in 607 AD, Japan has been struck by magnitude 7.0 or greater earthquakes almost fifty times. Yet the 122-foot-high (37 meter) structure remains standing. The reason: wood. The key to a building's ability to survive a massive earthquake is elasticity—and timber is one of most flexible building materials available. Lumber is plentiful in the Pacific Northwest. That's why builders are increasingly reaching for a material called CLT: cross-laminated timber. CLT is made by slathering sheets of timber with glue, heating them, and then pressing them together, with each layer turned ninety degrees from the layer below. Crossing the wood grains gives CLT the strength of steel. And results from testing at Oregon State's structural lab proves that CLT retains the elasticity needed to withstand Cascadia-size earthquake forces.

CLT does more than prepare the Pacific Northwest for earthquakes—timber harvests can be a boon for depressed rural areas. The material also speeds up construction time (because it can be precision-cut for assembly). It even addresses global climate change. Production of concrete and steel is responsible for roughly 8 percent of global greenhouse emissions. Trees pull carbon dioxide from the atmosphere—so skyscrapers built with timber actually act as carbon storage. It seems a stretch to call a building material a lifesaver, but in the Pacific Northwest, CLT could be just that.

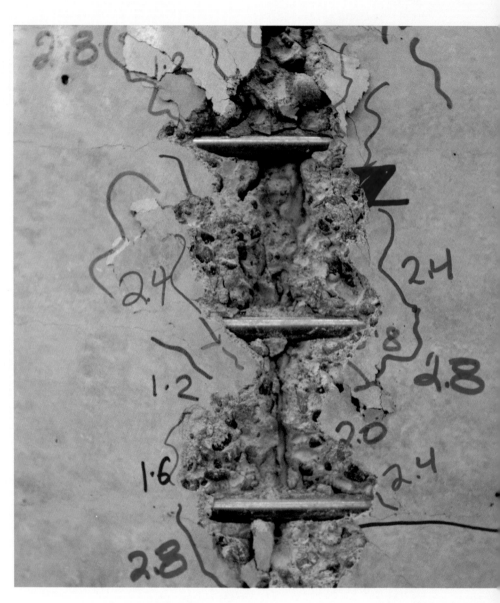

Before and After Retrofitting

Many old bridges in Oregon and across the Pacific Northwest contain this flaw uncovered in the test bridge column: instead of one length of rebar supporting the whole column, two shorter pieces of rebar are wrapped together. Once the splice fails during shaking, as it has in this photo, the bridge cannot sustain its weight and might collapse.

The rebar splice area of the retrofitted bridge column survived high amounts of movement—1.6 inches, 2.4 inches, even 2.8 inches—without displaying any damage to the rebar splice. The splice eventually failed at about 4 inches of displacement, but with the added support the column itself did not fail until much later.

about how columns like this would respond to a Cascadia earthquake," says Chris. "But we can say that this column failed with very little force and very little displacement. We would expect to see more of both in a large quake."

But Chris has a fix for the splice, a retrofit that Sharoo is going to test. Titanium, he thinks, is the key. Titanium has half the density of steel, but tons more strength. While rebar can support 60,000 pounds per square inch, titanium can handle an amazing 140,000 pounds per square inch. "Yes, titanium is more expensive than other kinds of materials used in retrofits, but it can do things that other materials cannot, and when you compare it to tearing down the bridge and rebuilding, the cost is minimal. Do we want to put on Band-Aids that might fail, or invest in retrofits that we know will perform—that will keep the bridge in service?" asks Chris. "The answer to me is obvious."

A few months later, Chris and Sharoo gather again to test the retrofit on another column. They have added titanium bars over the splice, which act like splints on a broken arm. Then they wrapped the area with a titanium coil and filled in the space with concrete to hold the column together, like a cast around a broken arm. "It's like orthopedic surgery for a bridge, but done before the fracture even happens," says Chris. "We can do this because we know the exact location of the weak point."

The team runs the retrofitted column through the same paces, pushing and pulling it fractions of an inch, a full inch, two inches, three inches, and four inches. At that point, the rebar splice finally fails. But that means it survived *more than four times* the displacement as the control column. And that's just the beginning.

The team proved that they had a way to ensure that bridges of the Pacific Northwest could survive a Cascadia quake.

According to sensors, the column is still structurally sound. So the engineers continue to push and pull it: five inches, six inches, seven inches, eight, nine, and ten. "That was well above what a bridge would face in a Cascadia quake," says Chris. "The titanium did an amazing job carrying the load. It was transformative. You'd be hard pressed to design a brand new column with that level of performance."

The team proved that they had a way to ensure that bridges of the Pacific Northwest could survive a Cascadia quake. "We can absolutely do it from an engineering sense," says Chris. "But do we have the political will and funding to make it happen? That is the question."

The aftershocks of the 2011 Japan earthquake that Chris Goldfinger experienced lasted for days, and the coast was tragically devastated by the tsunami. But inland, life resumed almost immediately. The day after the quake, Chris strolled to a bustling local farmer's market where he bought some pottery. "If you are in a resilient society," he says, "a big earthquake is just an exciting day."

And a little bit of warning can make everyone even safer.

STUDYING TSUNAMIS

At times during the bridge column test, the sounds of the creaks and cracks were overpowered by a large groan and the whooshing sound of water surging. That's because at the same time, under the same roof, another type of structural testing was happening—tsunami testing.

In the wave flume, a swell of water pushes two white plastic blocks (representing debris such as logs) toward an orange box wired with sensors (representing a coastal building). The sensors will measure the force of the impact the building sustains from the floating blocks.

Much is already known about how the force of water affects structures. This test was designed to explore how floating objects such as boats, cars, trucks, docks, trees, and even parts of buildings that are carried by tsunami surges might damage buildings.

"Large debris is just a reality of tsunamis," says Krishnendu (Krish) Shekhar, who is visiting the Oregon State wave flume with fellow graduate student Andrew Winter from the University of Washington in Seattle. They, along with postdoctoral scholar Mohommad Shafiqual Alam, have created computer models that suggest that where debris piles up against a building, the wall must endure forces five to ten times stronger than the force produced by the surging water. "That's an important fact to confirm," Andrew says. These tests will help corroborate and refine their computer programs so that engineers can better design buildings to withstand all that tsunamis might throw at them.

At one end of the 324-foot (104 meter) wave flume, the team has placed a large orange box with sensors representing a house or other building. Ten dense plastic blocks float in place nearby, racked together by a wooden frame.

"We want to know what kind of load buildings and bridges will have to sustain from debris," says Tori Johnson, a postdoc researcher at OSU. The team is also curious about how the debris will move. Will it strike and bounce off, causing a momentary load, or will the debris hit and stay pressed against

OSU researcher Tori Johnson wades into the wave flume to arrange plastic blocks that mimic debris that can strike a building during a tsunami.

the building, adding stress over a longer period of time?

When they are ready, Andrew dials up a wave from the control room. At the far end of the flume, there's a deep rumble as a large paddle generates the "tsunami."

When the swell nears the plastic blocks, Tori pushes a button, and a crane lifts the wooden frame, freeing the debris. The wave hits and the blocks rise and sweep toward the house. They strike, with the sound of a rapid-firing gun, *bang, bang, bang*. Two bump into each other, hit the corner of the building, and bounce off and around it. One turns sideways, and the force of the surge pushes it underwater and pins it to the building.

The researchers are pleased, as the debris strikes have surely registered on their sensors.

But they don't check the numbers. They have a long list of configurations to test. What if one block points right at the building? What if it hits the building on its long side? What if there are two, three, four, five, six blocks in these different configurations? How does the debris interact, jostling other pieces of wreckage or piling up alongside the house?

The team members slop into the flume in waders, grabbing stray debris, and placing the blocks in the proper arrangements for each test.

"It's my first time doing experimental work," says Krish. "It's cool to see things from the computer models tested in real conditions." And he and Andrew are eager to get back to their computers to add what they learn to their models. The survival of buildings and the people in them may depend on it.

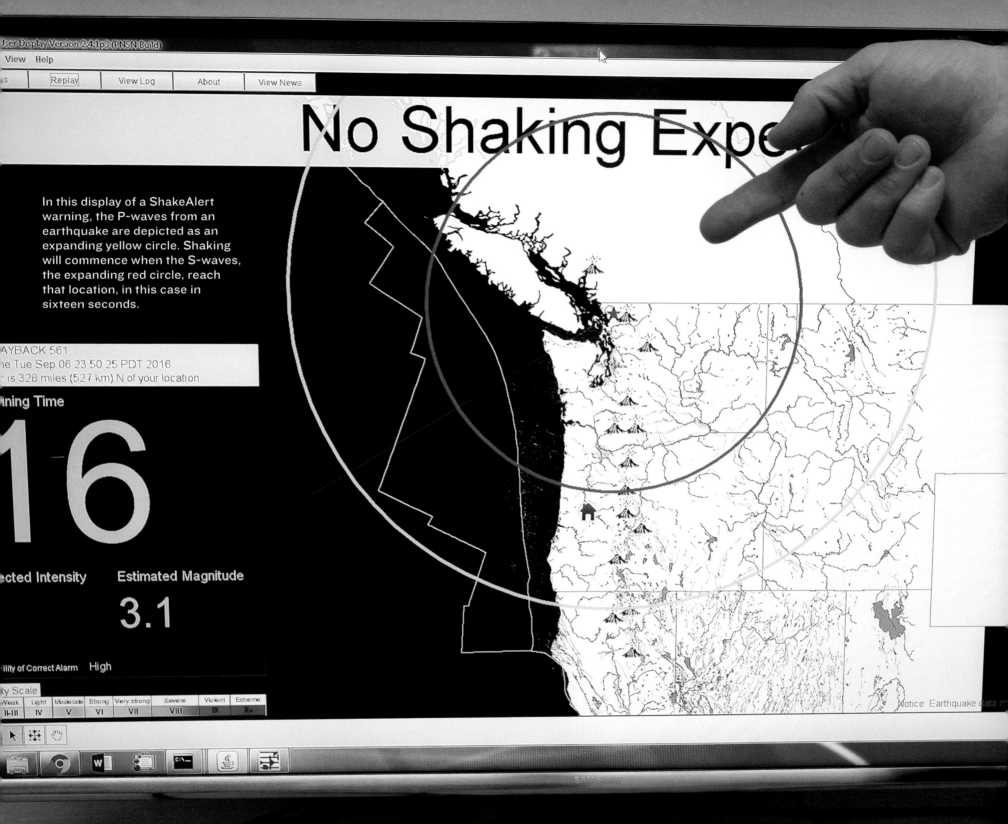

CHAPTER SEVEN
A LITTLE WARNING

WHAT IF WE KNEW ahead of time that a Cascadia earthquake was coming? Count to thirty. Thirty seconds is enough time to find a really safe place to drop, cover, and hold—maybe under a bed or under a big wooden desk in an adjacent room. Count thirty more seconds. A full minute might be enough time for a whole family or classroom to gather in the safest spot, ready to hunker down when the shaking begins. And just a couple minutes of warning is enough time to stop delicate medical procedures, open elevator doors, secure chemicals, even automatically slow or stop trains so they don't derail.

The scientists behind ShakeAlert are working to give everyone a few seconds to a few minutes' warning before the strongest shaking from a Cascadia earthquake hits.

Here's how: Scientists cannot yet predict a subduction zone earthquake—or any earthquake along a fault for that matter. But once an earthquake has begun, it sends out a distinct signal before the real shaking starts. The signal is called a P-wave, or primary wave. It is a pulse that moves outward in all directions, compressing the ground like an accordion as it goes. People are unlikely to feel this wave, but it can be detected by instruments called seismometers.

LOTS OF EARTHQUAKE STATIONS

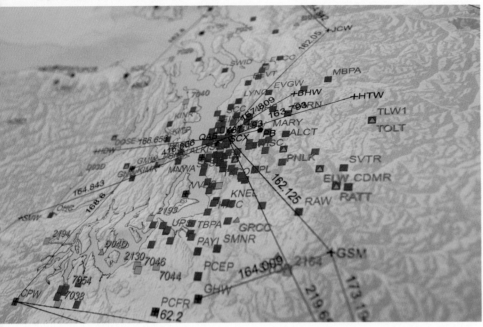

Locations of the many seismic stations around Puget Sound in Seattle.

NOT ENOUGH EARTHQUAKE STATIONS

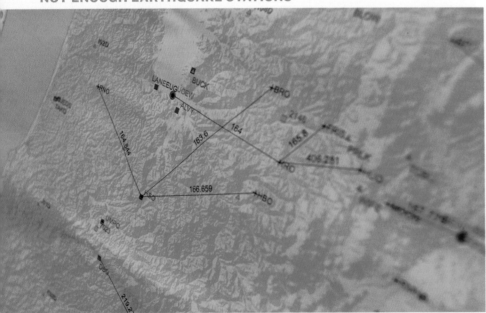

ShakeAlert scientists are working to build out the network of seismic stations in remote areas, such as this area in the Oregon coast range, where stations are too spread out for the system to effectively locate an earthquake.

P-waves are followed by the slower-moving secondary waves, or S-waves. The S-waves are the ones that violently buck the ground up and down and back and forth.

Near where the earthquake begins, called the epicenter, there is not much time between the P-waves and the S-waves. But as the P-waves spread quickly outward, the gap between the speedy P-waves and slower S-waves widens. This gap is the precious warning time.

Not long ago, when ShakeAlert was still being developed and tested, a 4.1 magnitude quake in Walterville, Oregon, triggered the system.

At the ShakeAlert lab at the University of Oregon, the computer blared out a long *BAAAAH,* then eight staccato noises: BAH, BAH, BAH, BAH, BAH, BAH, BAH, BAH.

"EARTHQUAKE! EARTHQUAKE!" a computerized male voice announced. "Weak. Shaking. Expected. In. Six. Seconds."

A map on a computer screen showed the yellow circle of the P-wave moving out from the epicenter and the red S-wave expanding outward afterward.

The alert continued, counting down until the S-wave arrived.

In this case, the earthquake was too small to cause any damage at the university. But that would not be the case if a massive Cascadia earthquake hit. The alert for a subduction zone quake would warn people to expect Moderate, Strong, Very Strong, Severe, Violent, or Extreme shaking.

The speed and accuracy of the system depend on being able to detect the P-wave as quickly as possible. Since no one knows where the subduction zone will first rupture, the scientists and engineers of ShakeAlert are building out a network of earthquake-detecting seismometers across the

The alert for a subduction zone quake would warn people to expect Moderate, Strong, Very Strong, Severe, Violent, or Extreme shaking.

ShakeAlert engineers head deep into the forest to repair a seismic station.

ShakeAlert engineers have to carry all their gear, including a step ladder, off trail through the forest to check on the Roman Nose seismic station.

ShakeAlert project manager Leland O'Driscoll (right) and technician Dennis Fletcher (left) check the electronics at the Roman Nose seismic station.

Pacific Northwest coastal region. "For the most effective early warning, we need seismometers roughly every twelve miles," says Leland O'Driscoll, ShakeAlert's project manager and a field seismologist at the University of Oregon.

That means putting in hundreds of new stations and maintaining and updating the hundreds of stations that were put in place before scientists even knew the danger the Cascadia earthquakes pose.

One such station is at Roman Nose, a hard-to-reach spot in the Oregon coast range. It has been giving the ShakeAlert team trouble over the last six months. "We keep losing the

signal," says Leland. Roman Nose is in an important location halfway between the coast and population centers along highway I-5, so they need it up and running. The next closest seismic station is more than thirty miles (48 kilometers) away.

So Leland gathers a team: field technician Dennis Fletcher; two geology graduate students, Miles Bodner and Brandon VanderBeek; and undergraduate Noel Blackwell.

They begin to gather materials. Duct tape. Sockets and wrenches. Electronic parts. Solar panel and casing. Battery.

With the trucks packed, the team hits the highway toward the coast. Eventually, the trucks head up a Forest Service road, through drizzle and thick fog. The road turns to dirt and the team bumps along until they are as close to the station as they can get.

They distribute the equipment and head straight into a scrubby forest, pushing through brush, climbing over fallen logs, ducking around trees. Wet branches and long weeds whip at their legs and arms. Someone slips and curses softly. Trees thicken.

They reach an area where volcanic rock has pushed through the softer soil. Here the ground is a jumble of lava rock, some jagged, some slick and covered with moss. Footsteps slow as everyone chooses a path from rock to rock. Miles's ladder gets tangled in the branches. He backs out. All conversation has ceased, and the only sounds are of water dripping off trees, twigs snapping, and low grunts when a team member gets snagged on something or lurches forward.

Suddenly, the forest parts. The team has reached a clearing. Before them is the Roman Nose station. Under what looks like a flagpole with an antenna and a flat solar panel sits a green metal box. The seismometer is actually not in the box—it's buried underground about twenty-five feet (8 meters) away from the rest of the station. "We don't want the seismometer to register movement caused by the solar mast blowing in the wind," says Leland.

Dennis immediately unlocks the box and places his handheld voltmeter on various instruments, checking to see how electricity is moving through the system. "I'm getting 15.92 watts from the solar but only 4.2 watts from the battery," he says. "So what is going on here? Why isn't power getting passed to the battery?"

Dennis and Leland put their heads together. "Maybe the wires are degraded," Leland suggests. "Let's follow the whole path." They bend over the box as if they are surgeons reaching into a patient. They trace the wires from the seismometer to the radio that transmits the signal and from the solar panel to the radio's battery.

When the Roman Nose station is working properly, it sends its signal forty-five miles (72 kilometers) to Harness Mountain near Cottage Grove, which relays it on to the University of Washington. The software at the university needs P-wave detection from three stations to calculate where the earthquake started (the epicenter), how big it is (the magnitude), how long before the shaking arrives at different locations, and how violent the shaking will be there. So every station is important.

All the wires and connections here look good. "Let's see what happens if we put a new battery in," Dennis says. But Leland is skeptical. "Even if that works, that's not the end of it," Leland says. "We've changed out the battery a few times already. The station works for a couple weeks, then goes dead."

They both stare up at the solar panel. "It's dinky, isn't it?" Dennis says.

"And old," Leland adds.

"We have to take it down."

The team grabs the solar mast and lifts it up and over onto its side until they can reach the solar panel. Before getting to work on it, though, they check the panel casing carefully for small, but potentially painful, hazards—scorpions, yellow jackets, and wasps—that may have moved in. "They love to make their nests up here," Leland says.

When they see it's clear, they go at the bolts with screwdrivers, but some are rusty and stuck. Twisting and banging as needed, they wrangle the old solar panel off. In a process that looks like building with a K'NEX kit, they make a case for the new solar panel. Finally, they wire the new panel in. While they work, the sun burns through the fog, and steam rises off their wet backs.

With all the equipment in place and wired, they push up the solar mast like it's a Christmas tree and turn the solar panel to face the sun.

It's the moment of truth. Leland and Brandon climb up the rubbly slope. Leland opens his laptop and fires it up. It looks like the seismometer is transmitting a signal. The vibrations from the scientists' footsteps register as little zigzags.

"Let's give it the test," Leland says.

And that means it's time to stomp. Miles heads over to stand on the ground right above the seismometer. *STOMP!* He waits. *STOMP STOMP!*

A few seconds go by.

If the station really is repaired, the seismometer underground will detect the ground movement and send the signal to the radio, which sends it out to the relay station in Cottage Grove, which transmits it to the University of Washington.

Five or six second later, Leland's laptop registers. ZIG. A big spike. Pause. ZIGZAG. Two more.

"All right!" Leland yells. "Data flow!"

It works.

But Leland doesn't like the delay. When a Cascadia earthquake hits, every second will count. "We need to get this delay down to one second," he says.

That's why ShakeAlert is in rapid expansion mode. In 2017, the early warning system had about 250 stations.

Leland O'Driscoll and graduate student Brandon VanderBeek (back) wait for a signal from the Roman Nose seismic station to reach their laptop from the relay station. ShakeAlert engineers want to shorten delay times so people will have as much early warning of earthquake shaking as possible.

Noel Blackwell (left), Miles Bodner (center), and Dennis Fletcher (right) push the new solar panel at Roman Nose upright.

"How effective would an early warning be if no one hears the warning and prepares?"

Ultimately, they want 560 stations in Oregon and Washington and another hundred in Northern California. "Ideally we would build out faster, but we are at the mercy of federal funding," Leland says.

The other big task is outreach. "We have to let people know what ShakeAlert is," Leland explains, "what it does, and why it matters. How effective would an early warning be if no one hears the warning and prepares?" ShakeAlert is currently testing the system with a limited rollout to partner organizations. They have plans to widen their reach to the public soon.

In Japan before the 2011 earthquake, the country's earthquake early warning system was the second most downloaded app in the country—after email.

"There is no doubt it saved lives," Leland says. "And ShakeAlert can, too."

Dan (left), Cloe (center), and Jasmine Scribner (right) examine backpacks filled with disaster supplies at the Friendly House in Portland, Oregon.

CHAPTER EIGHT

THE SCIENCE OF SAVING YOURSELF

WHAT SHOULD WE DO with our newfound knowledge of the danger the Cascadia Subduction Zone poses? Get ready!

All around the Pacific Northwest people have begun preparing. One warm June afternoon in Portland, Oregon, more than two hundred and fifty people from Willamette Heights gathered in the Friendly House community center gym to find out what steps they should take to be ready for a subduction zone earthquake. Neighbors preordered almost five hundred five-gallon water containers and purchased almost a hundred backpacks filled with disaster supplies.

Preparation is essential because while the vast majority of the millions of people who live in the shake zone will survive, many of the buildings, roads, and services people depend on may not. "The five to six minutes of shaking expected from a Cascadia earthquake means there will be lots of damage," Steven Eberlein, a Cascadia expert with the American Red Cross Cascades Region, told the Willamette Heights neighborhood gathering. "Much of our

BASIC EMERGENCY SUPPLY CHECKLIST

The United States Federal Emergency Management Agency (FEMA) suggests that you have this preparedness kit ready at home and anywhere else you spend a lot of time:

- Water, one gallon per person per day for at least three days
- Food, at least a three-day supply of nonperishable food (include a can opener if needed)
- Radio, hand cranked or battery powered with extra batteries
- NOAA weather radio with extra batteries
- First-aid kit
- Whistle to signal for help
- Dust masks to filter contaminated air
- Tent, tarp, or plastic sheeting and duct tape to make a shelter
- Moist towelettes, garbage bags, and plastic ties for sanitation
- Wrench or pliers to turn off utilities
- Local maps

There's more you and your parents can do to prepare. Visit the website of the American Red Cross Cascades Region at www.redcross.org/local/oregon/about-us/our-work.html to read and download its brochure and app "Prepare! A Resource Guide."

"When you are ready for a Cascadia earthquake, you will be ready for anything."

infrastructure could be destroyed, which means families will have to go without city water, electricity, and sanitation."

While getting ready is critical for people in the Pacific Northwest, it's a good idea for everyone, Steven says. Forty-five states, located in every region of the country, are at moderate to very high risk of earthquakes.

Home is the most important place to prepare simply because that's where you spend the most time. The great news is that most homes are made of wood and are expected to fare pretty well in an earthquake. "Wood flexes, so wooden houses may shift off their foundations but are not expected to collapse," says Steven.

Still, you need to get the interior ready and stock up with supplies. The first free and easy step is what Steven calls "a heavy and high" search. Walk around your home room by room. Imagine each room shaking hard for five minutes. Note any heavy objects placed high up, like on a shelf. These are objects that could fall and hurt someone. Move them lower.

Next gather supplies. Preparing for a disaster is a little like preparing for a camping trip. You want to have everything on hand that you might need. You may be able to stay in your home, but in case you can't, think about shelter. A shelter can be as fancy as a tent or as simple as a couple tarps and some rope or plastic garbage bags and duct tape.

Store some water, at least one gallon per person per day. "Go water crazy," says Steven. "You can't have too much."

Collect food with lots of calories that will last unrefrigerated and can be eaten uncooked. Think energy bars, canned beans, nut butters, dried meats. And don't forget food for your pet!

Consider that you might be without electricity for a while. Pack flashlights and batteries. Also, the weather is often cold and wet in the Pacific Northwest, so pack warm clothes, blankets, and ponchos or raincoats—even plastic garbage bags. "It would be great if the earthquake happened on a sunny day in the middle of June," Steven says, "but you have to be ready for it to happen anytime."

Assembling a disaster kit is something anyone of almost any age can do. Grab a duffle bag, backpack, or even an old pillowcase and fill it with items on hand. Make a list of what you can't find around the house. Your parents may be able to purchase the rest, or you can raise money to support the effort (babysit, mow lawns, do chores, or hold a bake sale or car wash). Store the supplies somewhere easily accessible to an exit in your home.

"One great part about being prepared is that once you're ready, you don't really have to think about it anymore," says Steven. "You can go on with your life and sleep well at night."

Planning for an earthquake also prepares you and your family for other natural disasters such as fires, tornadoes, hurricanes, and floods. "When you are ready for a Cascadia earthquake, you will be ready for anything," says Steven.

Teens help carry empty water containers to people's cars. Storing water is one of the most important steps in preparing for any natural disaster.

WHAT TO DO IF YOU ARE . . .

IN A WOOD, NEW, OR RETROFITTED BUILDING

DROP, COVER, AND HOLD

The first thing you'll feel is a short jolt. "Your instinct will be to go, 'Hey what was that? Did you feel that?' and stand around and talk about it. Don't," says Steven Eberlein. "That is your wake-up call to drop, cover, and hold." Specifically:

DROP: Before the shaking knocks you over, drop to the ground.

COVER: Crouch under a hard piece of furniture such as a desk or table. Think of it as a hard umbrella that can protect you from falling and flying objects.

HOLD: Grasp the furniture tightly or it can move away from you during the shaking. Stay there until the shaking stops.

IN AN OLD MASONRY BUILDING

MAKE A PLAN

Drop, cover, and hold is great advice when you are in newer, retrofitted, or wooden structures. But if you are in an unreinforced masonry building (like brick or stucco) that has a good chance of crumbling and collapsing, Chris Goldfinger suggests planning an escape route. Whether you leave during the earthquake or after, it's a good idea to know ahead of time where you're going. "Look at where you're actually sitting, how you're going to get out, and what could happen on the way out," he says. (Planning an exit route is especially important for those with limited mobility.)

Unlike earthquakes along the San Andreas Fault, which are quick and violent, subduction zone earthquakes start off small and gradually grow more powerful. "You have some time," says Chris. "So the question is, What are you going to do with that time? Have a plan that makes good use of it to get yourself into the safest place possible."

OUTSIDE OR IN A CAR

STAY PUT

If you are outside during an earthquake, find an open spot away from buildings, power lines, trees, or anything that could fall on you. Drop to the ground and stay there.

If you are in a car, stay with your seat belt fastened until the shaking stops. If a power line falls on your car, do not get out until help arrives.

You never know where you may be in the car when a quake hits, so it's a good idea to keep some disaster supplies in the trunk. "Grab a big Ziploc bag, throw in some granola bars, a couple ponchos, a whistle, a flashlight, and some water, and put it in your car," Steven suggests.

AT THE BEACH

HEAD TO HIGH GROUND

When Chris Goldfinger was visiting a coastal area in Japan destroyed by the 2011 tsunami, he spotted a very old sign that read: "If you build above this line, you'll have a long and happy life." Homes below the sign were demolished by the huge swells. Homes above survived unscathed.

The sign was correct. There is one sure way to survive a tsunami: head to high ground.

You will get a powerful warning—the earthquake. As soon as the shaking has stopped, immediately move as fast as you can to high ground. Moving to higher ground does not always mean heading inland. Surges of water can reach as far as a mile from the beach. You want to move up in elevation—fifty to one hundred feet (15 to 30 meters) above the shore. Follow tsunami evacuation signs or hike as high as you can up the nearest hill. If you don't see a hill, find a strong-looking building as high up and as far away from the beach as possible and head to the top floor or roof.

Move fast and don't carry anything that will slow you down. When you reach a safe height, stay put. The tsunami is likely to have multiple surges that can pour in over several hours. Do not return to lower ground until you are certain the danger has passed.

SEPARATED FROM YOUR FAMILY

REUNITE

You can't predict where you and your family will be if an earthquake happens, so make an emergency plan. If your family is not all in one place, where will you try to meet? "We suggest picking three locations," says Steven. "Perhaps your home, an alternate site in your neighborhood such as a park, and one spot outside your neighborhood in case your neighborhood is not safe."

It's a great idea to choose a contact person outside the Cascadia zone who can take messages and coordinate activities if you have a hard time communicating within the zone. Put the name and number with your disaster supplies, in your cellphone, in your family's car, and in your school backpack. Be aware that cellphone service may be disrupted or intermittent, so make sure everyone in the family knows what to do if they can't communicate by phone. "The more clear and specific your family plan, the better off you all will be," says Steven.

Luke Ohama pedals over the Tilikum Crossing bridge in Portland, Oregon, as part of the Disaster Relief Trials, a race that demonstrates the power of bikes in disaster relief.

CHAPTER NINE
DON'T BE SCARED; GET YOUR COMMUNITY PREPARED

"PREPARE OUT LOUD" is one of the mottos of the American Red Cross, the largest disaster relief organization in the United States. You and your whole neighborhood will be safer when everyone around you prepares. "Preparing is a community activity," says Steven. "Show people how you're preparing. Yes, even post it on Facebook or Instagram." Talk to your friends, classmates, teammates, and teachers about what you're doing to prepare. Have a friend over and prepare together. Organize a block party where families bring supplies to store together in a common shed.

Many classrooms and schools have taken steps to prepare, and yours should, too. For instance, Portland Public Schools has outfitted more than three thousand classrooms with

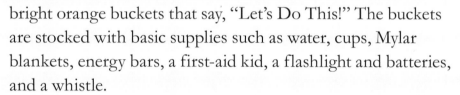

Teens Luke Ohama and Tanner Slechta tuck delicate raw eggs into their backpacks to represent fragile medicines that might need to be transported by bike after a Cascadia quake.

Luke lugs buckets of water hauled from the Willamette River, which his team will strap to their bike trailers and deliver across town.

bright orange buckets that say, "Let's Do This!" The buckets are stocked with basic supplies such as water, cups, Mylar blankets, energy bars, a first-aid kid, a flashlight and batteries, and a whistle.

Schools all over the region are also practicing earthquake drills. Some are taking it a step further and practicing how they will reunite students with their families after an earthquake. If your school has not begun to prepare, you can lead the effort. Talk with your parents, teachers, and principal about how to get started.

Some people, including young people, are training to be ready to help out if a Cascadia quake strikes. In a parking lot in downtown Portland, Oregon, Luke Ohama, age fifteen, Tanner Slechta, age sixteen, their dads, and their dads' friends have gathered at Disaster Relief Trials for that very reason. Their two teams sprint toward a pile of five-gallon buckets and some cartons of eggs. Luke and Tanner grab eggs, wrap

them in newspaper, pad them with sweatshirts, and nestle them into their backpacks. Their dads grab empty buckets and strap them to trailers on the back of their bikes.

The Disaster Relief Trials pretend that the worst has happened. The Cascadia Subduction Zone has unleashed seven minutes and twenty-five seconds of shaking, destroying roads, stores, and hospitals and damaging water and power lines.

Most of the bikers who have gathered for the trials have already prepared for themselves and their families—stashing food, clothing, first-aid kits, and ample water in their homes, cars, and workplaces. "I had a bunch of fun making plans for an imaginary zombie apocalypse," says team member Greg Dyer. "It translates pretty well to real-life prep."

Now they are practicing being ready to assist others.

The annual event, also held in Seattle, San Francisco, and Eugene, Oregon, begins with dozens of cargo bikes parked at one end of the lot and riders at the starting line at the other end. Organizer Emma Stoker describes the scenario of the imaginary Cascadia earthquake: "Neighbors need your help. Your task is to pick up and deliver supplies all across the city. All bridges have collapsed except Tilikum Crossing, so that is the only bridge you can use." (Tilikum is a new bridge, built to survive a Cascadia quake.)

They will carry eggs, representing fragile medical supplies. "We want to see these delivered safely, unbroken," Emma says. "And you'll need buckets to carry the gold." By gold she means water.

"Are you ready?"

"Set?"

"Go!"

And they're off!

They pedal fast in a line, weaving through city streets and up over the one functioning bridge that spans the Willamette River. They hop on a bike path that follows the river for about four miles (6.4 kilometers). With a light load, they ride fast. But before hitting any bumps, Luke and Tanner stand up on the pedals so the precious eggs/medicines don't get jostled.

They turn and coast down a steep hill to Sellwood Riverfront Park. There, they unstrap the buckets and carry them quickly over slippery cement and scoop them full of Willamette water. "Whoa," Luke mutters as he lifts the water buckets and stumbles with them, sloshing, back to the bikes.

After strapping the water buckets to the trailer, the team members consider the hill they had raced down. With about sixty pounds (27 kilograms) of extra weight now, there's only one way up: they have to push the bikes.

When they return to the Springwater bike path, the flat ride doesn't feel so flat anymore. After about four miles, the challenge ramps up. They climb, up, up, up a hill, panting, legs burning to a checkpoint in a city park. There, they "deliver" some water, which means dumping it down a drain. "It helps to pretend someone really needed it," Greg quips.

Feeling just a little lighter, they glide down the hill, yelling "Wheeee!" But at the bottom of the hill, the hollering stops as they lug cardboard boxes holding forty pounds (18 kilograms) of canned food to their bikes. "It's pretty satisfying to see how the trailer that I built from scratch is performing," says Sam, Tanner's dad. "It's entirely practical and usable for this situation."

Though the trailers are heavy, the riding is pretty easy for a while. But the route might not be that smooth in a real earthquake, with piles of rubble and widespread road damage. So the race includes some obstacles. All the teams have to get their bikes and cargo over an almost three-foot-high (1 meter) barrier—three times. This takes teamwork, muscle, and a fair amount of grunting.

And sometimes it takes helping another team that is just in front or just behind. "In the real thing, we would all be in this together," says Tanner.

Then the race grinds to a halt. As they drop Tanner's dad's bike over the last barrier, the hitch to the cargo trailer bends—and breaks. The team clusters around the broken part, studying the damage. Without a fix, the race is over for this team, which means water, food, and medicine will remain undelivered. But these riders are all about being prepared.

"I have some zip ties," says team member William Douglas.

"And I've got electrical tape," says Greg.

"And if we shift the weight to the front of the trailer, that will help keep it in place, too," Sam adds.

They get to work, wrapping and tying the hitch in place. "This is the kind of thing we'll have to be willing to do," says William. "We have to be ready to fix things, to live and learn."

Off they go, pedaling a dozen blocks through the city, with cars and the MAX train rushing by. Sam bikes carefully, avoiding bumps, and Luke and Tanner take turns following him to make sure the hitch holds.

In all the strain and excitement, it's easy to forget about the eggs—which represent precious medicine. As if remembering the eggs' fragility, the group pulls to a gentle stop in front of a tall building downtown. Luke and Tanner carefully take off their backpacks and dig out the sweatshirts that have cushioned the eggs. They laugh nervously about the mess they may have made. Then they unroll the newspaper. All eight eggs have survived intact.

"Yes!" Luke's dad, Joe, says.

There's no time to celebrate as food is needed six long miles (almost 10 kilometers) away. So off the two teams go, weaving through the industrial area, under highways, and over legions of potholes. The last stretch is another uphill grind, but the group soars down the hill after dropping off the heavy food. Luke pops wheelies and jumps curbs.

There's only one stop left before the finish, but it's a doozy. The bikers have to haul four shipping pallets—each 4 by 3½ feet (1.3 by 1 meter)—the rest of the way. Bulky and awkward, the pallets are challenging to strap on. And they are heavy, like hauling a couple bags of dog food. "But look how well the bike trailers would work in an actual disaster," Luke says.

The riders make their final wobbly way through the streets of Portland with the sun setting and air cooling. They ride gingerly, making sure not to scrape cars or bump into telephone poles with their wide loads.

As they pedal toward the finish line, they speed up. It's a hill, but they pump up it, faster and faster. It's been a long, tiring, but satisfying day, a day where they proved they are ready to help out wherever help is needed after a Cascadia earthquake.

Luke's and Tanner's teams raced for more than five hours, but finished in the rear of the pack. But the Disaster Relief Trials is a race in which everyone wins.

Team members were tired with sore legs, but they all had fun biking. Tanner would like to ride again next year. He laughs. "As long as I have a more comfortable seat!"

And Luke wants to haul a load on his own cargo bike. "I think I'm ready," he says.

Are you?

Greg Dyer (left), Luke (right), and his dad, Joe Ohama (center), struggle to strap pallets onto a bike trailer.

Tanner Slechta easily lifts his bike over one of the barriers on the Disaster Relief Trials path, proving how ready he is to help out after a Cascadia quake.

GLOSSARY

Aftershocks: smaller earthquakes that can happen hours, days, or even weeks after a major earthquake

Carbon dating: the process of estimating the age of organic material such as leaves and twigs by measuring the proportion of radioactive carbon-12 and carbon-14 in the material

Carbon fiber: a strong material made with carbon filaments

Cascadia Subduction Zone: the area around the North American tectonic plate boundary about fifty miles (80 kilometers) off the coast of the Pacific Northwest and stretching about six hundred twenty miles (1,000 kilometers) from Vancouver, British Columbia, in Canada to Northern California

Continent: a very large expanse of land usually encompassing multiple countries

Dendrochronologist: a scientist who studies the growth rings of trees to estimate a tree's age and the environmental conditions in which the tree lived

Earthquake: a violent shaking of the ground caused by geological processes

Elasticity: the ability of a material to return to its original shape after being stretched or bent

Engineer: a scientist who studies, designs, builds, tests, or alters buildings, structures, or machines

Epicenter: the place on the Earth's surface directly above where an earthquake began underground

Erosion: the process of wind, water, or chemicals altering, wearing away, or destroying objects or structures

Estuary: the mouth where a stream or river enters the sea; where fresh water meets tidal salt water from the ocean

Evacuate: to remove people or objects from a dangerous place

Fault: a crack in the Earth's crust forming the boundary between tectonic plates

Fossils: the remains or impression of a creature, plant, or object preserved in rock

Geological: relating to the Earth or the study of the Earth

Glacier: a mass of tightly compacted ice that survives year round

Greenhouse emissions: a gas such as carbon dioxide that warms the planet, often created by the burning of fossil fuels such as coal and oil

Gully: a narrow, steep-sided ravine formed by running water

Hypothesis: a proposed explanation based on observations that scientists will try to test

Infrastructure: the system of buildings, roads, bridges, and power plants that people nearby depend on

Landslide: the sudden movement of a mass of soil, rocks, mud, and other objects down a hillside or cliff

Marsh: low-elevation, waterlogged, often treeless land that can flood during high tides and rainstorms

Oceanography: the scientific study of oceans and their inhabitants

Paleoseismologist: a scientist who studies old and sometimes ancient earthquakes

Plate tectonics: a widely accepted theory that many geological phenomena are the result of large crustal plates moving on the Earth's mantle

Radiocarbon: a radioactive form of carbon

Retrofit: to add to or change an existing structure, often using newer technology

Rupture: the act or moment of breaking; an event that generates ground shaking along a fault; the portion of a fault that slips during an earthquake

Sediment: particles of mud, soil, or other matter carried by flowing water and deposited on the river or sea floor

Seismometer: an instrument that measures the force and duration of an earthquake; also called a seismograph

Subduction: the downward movement of a tectonic plate below another plate

Titanium: a strong, very hard, very lightweight metal that resists corrosion

Tsunami: a large wave or series of waves triggered by displacement of large amounts of water, often by ground movement during an earthquake

Turbidite: a deposit of sediment caused by a flow of water due to gravity

Voltmeter: an electronic instrument that measures, in volts, how much electricity could move between two points in a circuit

FURTHER READING

Atwater, Brian, et al. *The Orphan Tsunami of 1700: Japanese Clues to a Parent Earthquake in North America.* Seattle: University of Washington Press, 2015.

Barcott, Bruce. "Quakenami! Why the Pacific Northwest Is Doomed." *Outside Magazine,* August 25, 2011.

Doughton, Sandi. *Full-Rip 9.0: The Next Big Earthquake in the Pacific Northwest.* Seattle: Sasquatch, 2014.

Fradin, Judy and Dennis. *Earthquakes: Witness to Disaster.* Washington, DC: National Geographic, 2008.

Harris, Nicholas. *Earthquakes Through Time.* New York: PowerKids Press, 2009.

Jennings, Terry. *Earthquakes and Tsunamis.* Mankato, Minn.: Smart Apple Media, 2010.

Schulz, Kathryn. "The Really Big One." *New Yorker,* July 20, 2015.

Stewart, Melissa. *Inside Earthquakes.* New York: Sterling Children's Books, 2011.

FURTHER SURFING: WEBSITES AND VIDEOS

EARTHQUAKES

Eight-minute animation of how shaking would spread in a 9.0 Cascadia earthquake: *www.youtube.com/watch?v=613Mpre8Vzw*

Raw footage of shaking in the March 11, 2011, Japanese subduction zone earthquake on the fifth floor of a store in Tokyo: *www.youtube.com/watch?v=6gH3qT7XCOE*

See the most recent earthquakes around the world at Earthquake Track: *earthquaketrack.com/v/pnw/recent*

TEDx talk by Chris Goldfinger: *www.youtube.com/watch?v=Iy5a2P3zXl4*

ENGINEERING AND RESEARCH

Cascadia Lifelines Program: *cascadia.oregonstate.edu*

M9: *hazards.uw.edu/geology/m9*

Oregon State University Structural Research: *cce.oregonstate.edu/structural-research*

PREPAREDNESS

American Red Cross Cascades Region: *www.redcross.org/local/oregon/preparedness*

Disaster Relief Trials: *disasterrelieftrials.com*

SHAKEALERT

Get updates and the app when it is ready: *www.shakealert.org*

Video of how ShakeAlert works: *www.youtube.com/watch?v=WWl3m4OyU44&feature=youtu.be*

Simulation of ShakeAlert warning for an 8.0 Cascadia earthquake: *www.youtube.com/watch?v=U-oqteTe-O4*

TSUNAMIS

Animation of the 1700 tsunami traveling from the Pacific Northwest to Japan: *www.youtube.com/watch?v=4W2iUl0VB8c&feature=youtu.be*

Put in an address and find tsunami evacuation maps: *nvs.nanoos.org/TsunamiEvac*

SOURCES

Alam, Mohommad Shafiqual. Postdoctoral scholar, School of Civil and Construction Engineering, Oregon State University, Corvallis, Oregon. In-person interviews and observation, OSU structural lab, 2017.

Alam, M. S., et al. "Tsunami-like Wave Induced Lateral and Uplift Pressures and Forces on an Elevated Coastal Structure." *Journal of Waterway, Port, Coastal, and Ocean Engineering* (in press).

American Red Cross Cascades Region. *Prepare! A Resource Guide.* www. redcross.org/local/oregon/preparedness/resource-guide

Atwater, Brian F. Affiliate Professor, Earth and Space Sciences, University of Washington, Seattle, Washington, and USGS research scientist. In-person interviews and observation, Nestucca River, 2017.

Atwater, Brian F., et al. *The Orphan Tsunami of 1700: Japanese Clues to a Parent Earthquake in North America.* Seattle: University of Washington Press, 2015.

Barbosa, Andre. Assistant Professor, Civil and Construction Engineering, Oregon State University, Corvallis, Oregon. In-person interviews and observation, OSU structural lab, 2017.

Barcott, Bruce. "Quakenami! Why the Pacific Northwest Is Doomed." *Outside Magazine,* August 25, 2011.

Blackwell, Noel. BS candidate and assistant, Department of Earth Sciences, University of Oregon, Eugene, Oregon. In-person interviews and observation, Roman Nose seismic station, 2016.

Bodner, Miles. PhD candidate, Department of Earth Sciences, OU Seismic Lab, University of Oregon, Eugene, Oregon. In-person interviews and observation, Roman Nose seismic station, 2016.

Booth, Adam M., et al. "Holocene History of Deep-Seated Landsliding in the North Fork Stillaguamish River Valley from Surface Roughness Analysis, Radio Carbon-Dating, and Numerical Landscape Evolution Modeling." *Journal of Geophysical Research Earth Science* 122: 456–72.

Burkett, Erin R., et al. *ShakeAlert—An Earthquake Early Warning System for the United States West Coast.* USGS Fact Sheet 2014-3083. U.S. Geological Survey, 2014.

Cascadia Region Earthquake Workgroup. *Cascadia Subduction Zone Earthquakes: A Magnitude 9.0 Earthquake Scenario.* Cascadia Region Earthquake Workgroup, 2013.

Clark, Douglas. Associate Professor, College of Science and Engineering, Western Washington University, Bellingham, Washington. In-person interviews and observation, Rowan landslide, 2016.

Doughton, Sandi. *Full-Rip 9.0: The Next Big Earthquake in the Pacific Northwest.* Seattle: Sasquatch, 2014.

———. "How Often Does Cascadia Fault Rip? Scientists Disagree." *Seattle Times,* August 9, 2014.

Douglas, William. Disaster Relief Trials entrant. In-person interviews and observation by bike. October 2016.

Duvall, Alison. Assistant Professor, Department of Earth and Space Sciences, University of Washington, Seattle, Washington. In-person interviews and observation, Rowan landslide, 2016.

Dyer, Greg. Disaster Relief Trials entrant. In-person interviews and observation by bike. October 2016.

Eberlein, Steven. Chief Development Officer, American Red Cross Cascades Region. In-person interview, Chapman School and Friendly House preparedness events, 2016.

Emmons, Molly. Emergency Preparedness Manager, Portland Public Schools. In-person interview, Chapman School and Friendly House preparedness events, 2016.

Federal Emergency Management Agency. Emergency Supply List. 2014. www.fema.gov/media-library/assets/documents/90354

Finkbeiner, Ann. "The Great Quake and the Great Drowning." *Hakai Magazine: Coastal Science and Societies,* September 14, 2015.

Fletcher, Dennis. Field Technician, ShakeAlert, University of Oregon, Eugene, Oregon. In-person interviews and observation, Roman Nose seismic station, 2016.

Goldfinger, Chris. Director, Active Tectonics and Seafloor Mapping Laboratory and professor of geology and geophysics, College of Earth, Ocean and Atmospheric Sciences, Oregon State University, Corvallis, Oregon. In-person and phone interviews and emails, 2016, 2017, and 2018.

Hassett, Whitney. Tillamook Bay Watershed Council, Tillamook, Oregon. In-person interviews and observation, Nestucca River, 2017.

Higgins, Christopher. Cecil and Sally Drinkward Professor of Structural Engineering, School of Civil and Construction Engineering and Director, Structural Engineering Research Laboratory at Oregon State University, Corvallis, Oregon. In-person interviews and observations, OSU structural lab, 2017.

Humboldt Earthquake Education Center. *Living on Shaky Ground: How to Survive Earthquakes and Tsunamis in Oregon.* Arcata, CA: Humboldt Earthquake Education Center, Humboldt State University, 2009.

Johnson, Tori. Postdoctoral Fellow, Oregon State University, Corvallis, Oregon. In-person interview and observations, OSU wave flume, 2017.

LaHusen, Sean. Graduate student, Department of Earth and Space Sciences, University of Washington, Seattle, Washington. In-person interviews and observation, Rowan landslide, 2016.

Lubick, Naomi. "Brian Atwater: Earthquake Hunter in the Field." *Geotimes,* August 2005. www.geotimes.org/aug05/profiles.html; accessed June 2017.

Ludwin, Ruth S., et al. "Dating the 1700 Cascadia Earthquake: Great Coastal Earthquakes in Native Stories." *Seismological Research Letters* 76, no. 2 (March/April 2005): 140–48.

Malick, Geoff. Graduate student, College of Science and Engineering, Western Washington University, Bellingham, Washington. In-person interviews and observation, Rowan landslide, 2016.

Manuel, Chris and Ruby. Disaster Relief Trials entrants. In-person interviews and observation by bike. October 2016.

O'Driscoll, Leland. Project Manager and Field Seismologist, ShakeAlert, University of Oregon. In-person interviews and observation, Roman Nose seismic station, 2016.

Ohama, Joe and Luke. Disaster Relief Trials entrants. In-person interviews and observation by bike. October 2016.

Paci-Green, Rebekah, et al. *Exercise Scenario Document, Cascadia Subduction Zone (CSZ), Catastrophic Earthquake and Tsunami.* Resilience Institute, Western Washington University. January 2015.

Roering, Josh. Professor of Earth Sciences, University of Oregon, Eugene, Oregon. In-person interviews and observation, Klickitat Lake, 2017.

Russell, Robert. Tillamook Bay Watershed Council, Tillamook, Oregon. In-person interviews and observation, Nestucca River, 2017.

Schulz, Kathryn. "The Really Big One." *New Yorker,* July 20, 2015.

Sexton, Jay. Research sawyer and senior research assistant with the Department of Forest Science, Oregon State University, Corvallis, Oregon. In-person interviews and observation, Klickitat Lake, 2017.

Shekhar, Krishnendu. Graduate student, University of Washington. In-person interview and observations, OSU wave flume, 2017.

Shlossman, Amy. Chief Executive Officer, American Red Cross Cascades Region. In-person interview, Chapman School and Friendly House preparedness events, 2016.

Shrestha, Sharoo. Graduate student, Department of Civil and Construction Engineering, Oregon State University, Corvallis, Oregon. In-person interviews and observation, OSU structural lab, 2017.

Slechta, Tanner and Sam. Disaster Relief Trials entrants. In-person interviews and observation by bike. October 2016.

Stewart, Melissa. *Inside Earthquakes.* New York: Sterling Children's Books, 2011.

Struble, Will. PhD candidate, Department of Earth Sciences, University of Oregon, Eugene, Oregon. In-person interviews and observation, Klickitat Lake, 2017.

VanderBeek, Brandon. PhD candidate, Department of Earth Sciences, University of Oregon, Eugene, Oregon. In-person interviews and observation, Roman Nose seismic station, 2016.

Winter, Andrew. Graduate student, Department of Civil & Environmental Engineering, University of Washington, Seattle, Washington. In-person interview and observations, OSU wave flume, 2017.

Wisehart, Susan. Graduate student, Department of Earth and Space Sciences, University of Washington, Seattle, Washington. In-person interviews and observations, Rowan landslide, 2016.

QUOTATIONS

The vast majority of quotations in the book are from in-person and follow-up interviews with the quoted sources. The exceptions are:

17 *In the days before the white man:* Ludwin, "Dating the 1700," 143.

 There was a big flood: Ibid., 142.

18 *They had practically no way:* Ibid., 142–43.

 I often joked: Lubick, "Brian Atwater," 1.

 Within Kuwagasaki village: Atwater, *The Orphan Tsunami,* 38–39.

 High tide or something: Ibid., 78–79.

PHOTO CREDITS

Natalie Behring: title page, iv, 7 (top left), 24 (bottom left), 34, 35, 36, 40, 42, 44 (right)
Erin Fitzpatrick-Bjorn: 4
Courtesy of Chris Goldfinger: 25, 26, 27
Sarah Harrington: 10, 12 (right), 13, 14, 56, 59, 62, 64, 66, 67
Houghton Mifflin Harcourt: 6 (top right and bottom right), 8, 9, 12 (top left), 21
Houghton Mifflin Harcourt (based on a graphic by Brian Atwater): 12 (bottom left)
Houghton Mifflin Harcourt (based on a graphic from NOAA): 24 (top right)
Houghton Mifflin Harcourt (based on a graphic by Massimo Pietrobon): 6 (left)
Anna Hoye: 41, 44 (left), 46, 47, 48, 50, 51, 52, 54, 55
JIJI PRESS/AFP/Getty Images: 3
Lamont-Doherty Earth Observatory and the estate of Marie Tharp: 7 (top right)
Hannah Letinich: 28, 30, 31, 32, 33
Chris McGrath/Staff, Getty Images News: 2
Naval History and Heritage Command: 7 (bottom)
Scott Olson/Getty Images: 38
Petrusbarbygere: 20
Paul Souders: 22
USGS: 37
Wikimedia Commons/Seattle Art Museum: 16
Wikimedia Commons/University of British Columbia Library: 19
© Yai/Shutterstock: copyright page

APPRECIATION

It will take the whole community to prepare for a Cascadia Subduction Zone earthquake. And it took a whole community to create this book. Thank you to my tireless intern, Elizabeth Goss, for all her background and photo research and for generally being willing to follow any lead I suggest. Thanks, too, to my two wonderful critique groups, the Viva Scrivas and the Downtown Group, for enduring any nightmares, literary or otherwise, that this manuscript may have provoked. Thanks to my three awesome Houghton editors, Amy Cloud, Cynthia Platt, and Erica Zappy Wainer. The book is so much stronger for all your contributions.

My deep appreciation to the talented photographers (Natalie Behring, Sarah Harrington, Anna Hoye, and Hannah Letinich) who followed me and the scientists into the field, sinking into muddy lakes, sliding down slippery banks, and getting tangled in brambles, all to get the perfect shot. Thanks, too, to photo editor and toning whiz Karin Anderson. The book is more beautiful for your work.

Finally, I want to thank all the scientists for allowing me to tag along on their fieldwork and for answering countless questions as I tried to make sense of my scribbled notes back home.

I also want to thank you for your important work. I rest easier at night knowing that you're studying the Cascadia Subduction Zone and the dangers it poses with such rigor and passion. We in the Pacific Northwest are lucky to have you.

INDEX

SCIENTISTS IN THE FIELD

Where Science Meets Adventure

Check out these titles to meet more scientists
who are out in the field—and contributing every day
to our knowledge of the world around us:

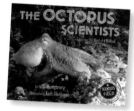

Looking for even more adventure? Craving updates on the work of your favorite scientists,
as well as in-depth video footage, audio, photography, and more? Then visit the Scientists in the Field website!

sciencemeetsadventure.com